DAILY MEDITATIONS FOR CHRISTIANS

DAILY
MEDITATIONS
for CHRISTIANS

A Year of Quotes, Reflections, and Scriptures

REBECCA HASTINGS

ROCKRIDGE
PRESS

Scripture quotations marked CSB have been taken from the Christian Standard Bible®, Copyright © 2017 by Holman Bible Publishers. Used by permission. Christian Standard Bible® and CSB® are federally registered trademarks of Holman Bible Publishers.

Interior and Cover Designer: Sean Doyle
Art Producer: Janice Ackerman
Editors: Adrienne Ingrum and Daniel Grogan
Production Editor: Nora Milman
Cover Illustration: Alek_Koltukov/istock
Author Photo: © 2019 Abigail Scott Photography

ISBN: Print 978-1-64152-874-0 | eBook 978-1-64152-875-7
R0

For Andrew, who always believes in me

INTRODUCTION

I HAVE BEEN CHANGED BY THE WORDS I'VE READ.
Like the time I held a thick book in my hands, and I turned the pages slower and slower because I didn't want the story to end. The book was *Redeeming Love*, and it showed me the love of God. Years later, I stood in front of a classroom, teaching fourth graders the magic of a great story. We came to know Aslan together and were captivated by the beauty of his grace and power in *The Lion, the Witch and the Wardrobe*. Staying up late into the night as my family slept, I read of a fictional prodigal in *Long Way Gone* who reminded me that God loves me no matter how far I run.

These stories changed me. They made me understand, wonder, and feel, transforming me as much as I let them. In time, those transformations became part of me.

Great fiction has brought me closer to God. And it can do the same for you. This book that you're holding in your hands is special because it combines powerful fiction with God's Word to help you grow closer to the Lord each day.

I meditate on God's Word because I desperately want peace for my soul. Everything around me feels busy. I'm not even talking about my calendar (although that is fuller than I'd like). I'm talking about all the things screaming for my attention.

It always seems there is more to do, more to see, and more to think about. It's as if I'm on a train that keeps going faster, so everything around me is a blur of lights and colors. They may be beautiful, but they don't lead to peace.

I want to have moments of stillness and focus on truth. I want to take time, even just a few moments, to fix my eyes on Jesus in the middle of all the busy. I want to feel a shift in my spirit from chaos to calm.

You, too?

When we spend time meditating on scripture, we know and understand God better. This gives our souls the peace and hope we're longing for.

Think about what you're facing today. Maybe it's a worry that has burrowed deep in your heart or the loss of someone you love. Maybe it's a season of struggle or illness or even blessing. Maybe it's just the deep knowing that you need something more.

I hope this book will offer you moments of soul-nourishing pause amid whatever struggle or circumstances are vying for your attention.

Intentionally short, these daily entries offer an inspiring quote from a work of fiction; a reflection, prayer, or affirmation; and a scripture for meditation. When we intentionally spend time with God, meditating on the Word, we grow. It doesn't need to be complicated to draw us to the heart of God.

Writing this book has changed me. I have been inspired, challenged, and encouraged. But more than anything, I have been reminded of God's deep, unending love for me. I have learned that meditating on the Word is the only way to find what I am truly longing for. That daily practice of time with the Lord has the power to change everything.

My prayer is that you will discover more of who God is from these writers and, as you turn these pages each day, you will be transformed by their words and the Word.

How I love your instruction! It is my meditation all day long.
—Psalm 119:97 CSB

1 God Speaks to Me

Whenever you are willing to obey me, Much-Afraid, and to follow the path of my choice, you will always be able to hear and recognize my voice, and when you hear it you must always obey. Remember also that it is always safe to obey my voice, even if it seems to call you to paths which look impossible or even crazy.

—*Hinds' Feet on High Places*, Hannah Hurnard

Despite the noisy distraction of the world, I will pursue God with assurance that the Lord knows and speaks to me.

MEDITATE ON JOHN 10:27

---

2 We Don't Always Understand, but We Have Hope

"There has to be a reason [Julian Goetz is dead.]"
"Oh, yes, there's a reason. There are a million reasons. But none of them matter one single iota unless you can fall on Jesus, wrap your arms around his neck, and weep."
"I don't know what that means."
"It means . . . hope isn't an explanation. It's a person."

—*Still Life*, Christa Parrish

We can find our hope in God no matter what we face. I will seek the Lord who offers the hope I am looking for.

MEDITATE ON PSALM 71:1–5

---

3 Jesus Knows My Pain

She didn't understand how it worked. She didn't understand why people starved to death and children ended up in orphanages while barren women longed for babies. She didn't understand why a cigarette break could save one person's life while driving home to get your daughter's hair bow could snatch another's. She would never understand why those people. Why that train. Why her.

But maybe she'd been asking the wrong question.

Maybe comfort wasn't found in the why.

Maybe comfort was to be found in the who.

A God who wept.

—*Life After,* Katie Ganshert

Jesus knew pain, felt loss, and wept when His friend died. Instead of trying to figure out why there is heartache, I invite Jesus into the painful places to receive His comfort and companionship.

MEDITATE ON JOHN 11:33–35

---

4 Sometimes the Small Things Are the Most Beautiful

"I guess that's what life is, though, isn't it? A whole bunch of little moments that don't seem significant or life-altering at the time, but when you look back . . ." She shook her head. "I don't know. They become the most profoundly beautiful things."
—*Life After*, Katie Ganshert

The ordinary, mundane events in life don't seem to amount to much each day, but no moment is insignificant to God. In all I do I will use my faithfulness to grow something beautiful.

MEDITATE ON MATTHEW 13:32
---

5 Linger in the Hard Places

"Remember, Charissa—the things that annoy, irritate, and dis-appoint us have just as much power to reveal the truth about ourselves as anything else. Learn to linger with what provokes you. You may just find the Spirit of God moving there."
—*Sensible Shoes: A Story About the Spiritual Journey*,
Sharon Garlough Brown

When something feels uncomfortable, we often think it isn't from God. There is peace in knowing my trials and annoy-ances can show me beautiful things about God.

MEDITATE ON 1 PETER 1:6–7
---

6 I Just Want to Know God's Will

She had challenged his whole life plan—to find God's will and do it—said he was fixated on finding the one thing God intended for him, when every moment was an opportunity. What if she was right? Could one choice be God's will, and another as well? It might not be about finding the one right answer as much as knowing the heart of God and choosing from the possibilities.

—*Secrets,* Kristen Heitzmann

I will spend five minutes sitting quietly in the presence of God without asking for anything. I will use the time to meditate on who God is.

MEDITATE ON MICAH 6:8

---

7 God Is Faithful

I couldn't find the words. Words to tell him how I had come to know a God as solid as this rock we stood upon. Unchanging, even after years of rain or snow or storm. Never swayed by even my own wavering heart. How He'd filled up a hole within me—a great need I hadn't even known existed until all I valued had been stripped bare.

—*The Edge of Mercy,* Heidi Chiavaroli

I will praise God for His faithfulness today, choosing to trust the everlasting Lord even when I am uncertain.

MEDITATE ON ISAIAH 40:28

---

8 Go to God First

It would be all too easy to rely upon her for strength, to turn to her to help him through his difficulties. But that wouldn't be fair to her. And it wouldn't be what God wanted either.

God wanted him to go to Him with his deepest needs, to stop looking elsewhere, so that he could be made whole again.

—*Hearts Made Whole*, Jody Hedlund

Instead of first going to others when we struggle, we should remember we have access to help of limitless power. I will go first to the Lord with all my needs.

MEDITATE ON 2 CHRONICLES 14:11

---

9 I Can Find Joy and Peace in Crisis

"Laughing together was so healing for Conrad and me!" she told us. "In fact, it helped prepare us for what lay ahead when he was diagnosed with pancreatic cancer. They couldn't operate—the cancer was too far advanced by the time he was diagnosed. But God showed us that even in the midst of a crisis, we can look for His gifts of joy and peace."

—*The Yada Yada Prayer Group*, Neta Jackson

I can find hope, even as I walk through troubles. I trust God to show me gifts of joy and peace in the midst of these hard circumstances.

MEDITATE ON 2 CORINTHIANS 4:18

---

10 My Words Will Spread Light

"What we say, my child, has an impact on those around us. Words can spread darkness and hate or shed light and love. Don't misuse them, Daphne."

—*A Matter of Character,* Robin Lee Hatcher

Words can escape our lips before we really think about the impact they have. I ask God to forgive me for things I've said today that are not full of light and love.

MEDITATE ON PROVERBS 18:4

---

11 Fully Serving God

I've done everything for the wrong reasons. All the good works people credit to me are nothing because I did them expecting God to repay me. I thought if I worked hard enough, God would have to give me what I wanted. The truth is I've never served the Lord at all. I was always serving myself.

—*As Sure as the Dawn,* Francine Rivers

There are times we act out of ambition or in seeking recognition instead of for God's glory. I am grateful for God's grace to forgive me and show me how to serve Him.

MEDITATE ON PSALM 90:17

---

12 Using My Gifts Well

Then I remember it is my God who gave me the desire and ability to do what I do . . . I give them a window through my camera. I don't capture landscapes or weddings or toddlers on Santa's lap. My photographs—I hope—bring the viewer to the doorstep of the divine, stirring them not only to compassion but to action.

—*Still Life,* Christa Parrish

We are called to live in compassion. I will be aware of those around me, using my gifts to show them kindness and love.

MEDITATE ON COLOSSIANS 3:12

13 Putting Love into Action

"Este es el amor con las piernas." She then translated without being asked. "'This is love with legs.' My father used to say that you can tell someone you love them until you're blue in the face, but until they see that walked out, they have no idea what it means. Hence, 'love with legs.'"

—*Water from My Heart,* Charles Martin

Think of three ways you can be "love with legs" for someone today.

MEDITATE ON LUKE 10:25–37

14 When God Feels Heavy

Josiah Rush was a few steps from his door when the Spirit of God fell upon him. His knees buckled. He fell backwards, sprawling helplessly on the ground, and stared up at the night sky.

It was a crushing weight. He couldn't breathe.

Like Gideon, he felt he would die.

Like Daniel, his anguish was unbearable.

Like Mary, he was gripped with fear.

Like Isaiah, he felt undone and unworthy.

Holiness covered him. The stench of his own sin was suffocating.

A presence surrounded him. Penetrated him. Linking him to eternity.

—*Fire,* Bill Bright and Jack Cavanaugh

The Holy Spirit is both beautiful and convicting. I invite the Spirit of God to penetrate my spirit today.

MEDITATE ON JOHN 16:7–15

---

15 Pathways of Understanding

"The memories are always with us, but sometimes we can ease the way for others. That is what we must do, use our pain to build understanding and empathy, not to build walls. Then it is transformed into a thing of beauty, then our suffering has value."

"That's a beautiful way to look at it," I say, capping the bottle and watching him closely.

"It's beautiful because it is true," Abel says.

—*The Enlightenment of Bees,* Rachel Linden

Lord, please soften the hard places in me, that they would become pathways to understanding and empathy toward others.

MEDITATE ON HEBREWS 6:10

16 The God of Bridges

I shielded my eyes with my hand, and I could see Nick's face. It was strained, as it had been for so long. I waved to him. He let himself smile, with a sadness and a longing I could almost hold in my hand.

"Just pray, Tristan," I said. "Pray that God would bridge the gap between what each of us has and what each of us needs to just be."

—*Tristan's Gap,* Nancy Rue

God is able to restore what seems ruined. I ask God to bridge the gap in relationships I am struggling with.

MEDITATE ON ISAIAH 61:4

17 Through the Worst

"This is a fallen world." The words sounded trite, impossibly small. "I hate that it's true, but there are diseases and poverty and suffering. A lot of it's unfair."

His profile hardened.

"He never promised us that we wouldn't suffer. But He's too just not to redeem it. And He does promise us that He won't leave us. That He'll be with us through the worst. That He loves us."

—*My Stubborn Heart*, Becky Wade

Father, help me trust that You are holding my hand in all that I face. Remind me of Your Spirit, that You never leave me.

MEDITATE ON ISAIAH 41:10

18 Giving Jesus Everything

Do everything as if unto the Lord. Offer up everything as if for the Lord, including jars of olives to the food pantry or leftover loaves of bread. Years later, that's finally how I make sense of it, where it settles out for me. If Jesus knocks on my door today, will I rummage through my home and give him the food I don't like, the outgrown jackets with stains and a broken zipper, the dirty Crock-Pot in the basement, the one with the chipped lid and mice nesting inside I've yet to find time to toss into the Salvation Army's dumpster?

—*Stones for Bread*, Christa Parrish

God deserves more than my leftovers. I will bring my best today to honor the Lord.

MEDITATE ON MALACHI 1:6–14

19 Freedom from Judgment

Cora's jovial expression gradually turned more serious. "Honey, one of these days you'll figure out that your heavenly Father isn't much like your earthly father. I'm sorry to say somethin' harsh about your daddy, but it's just the plain truth. God loves you, and He's not judgin' you." She reached over and patted my arm.

—*Inescapable*, Nancy Mehl

God loves me with perfect love and has set me free from judgment!

MEDITATE ON ROMANS 8:1-2

---

20 I Am Dear to Jesus

"Because . . . nothing worthwhile in life is free," Balint said. "When it costs something, that item becomes much dearer. Yes, the Word could have saved all of mankind by just His words, but instead He chose to heal mankind in a different way, by taking on the hurt and darkness Himself. And in doing so, we realize just how dear we are to Him."

—*Daughter of Light*, Morgan L. Busse

I am free from hurt and darkness because Jesus took all of it on my behalf. I am so deeply loved by Jesus that I can walk in complete mercy and freedom!

MEDITATE ON MARK 10:45

---

21 Life Changes, God's Word Does Not

She remembered Rebecca had been a beauty—small and delicate. It was plain to see how much she and Jonah loved each other. She had thought they were the luckiest two people on earth . . . until the accident.

As she thought about all Bertha had told her today, she found it hard to believe. But life could be like that, she had learned. A single decision, a moment in time, and the ground could shift beneath your feet.

—*The Search,* Suzanne Woods Fisher

When life around me is shifting and uncertain, I remember that God's Word is eternal. The Lord will always be faithful in my life.

MEDITATE ON ISAIAH 40:8

22 Bringing My Feelings to God

*Her mother had always said to be thankful for everything . . . or did she say be thankful **in** everything? Either way, Cassie was having trouble with the whole idea. Yes, she believed Jesus Christ died for her sins. Yes, she believed God loved her. But if this whole fiasco was His idea of love . . .*

—*Valley of Dreams,* Lauraine Snelling

I can bring all my feelings to God, moving forward in faith, trusting the Lord understands and will show me grace.

MEDITATE ON HEBREWS 4:14–15

23 Unwavering Belief

"You're young, Alex. And sometimes people get the feeling that maybe you haven't figured out whether you're totally committed to this. People want to follow someone with convictions, not questions. Smooth eloquence can never take the place of unwavering belief."

—*Fatal Convictions*, Randy Singer

The Lord longs for me to be committed fully, believing all the Word says in faith. May I be one of unwavering conviction, that the Lord may be glorified through me.

MEDITATE ON GALATIANS 6:9

24 Follow God's Heart

The thing is done; it can't be undone. How can one go back and change a moment passed? Even a moment that should never have come. I fear with the deed I have lost not only my virtue but my life as well. For of all life's betrayers, the heart is the worst. It flutters with joyful anticipation, leading down paths better untrod. Now that I know my heart, I must never follow it again.

—*The Rose Legacy*, Kristen Heitzmann

Ask God to show you the places in your heart that are not trustworthy so He can fill those places with truth.

MEDITATE ON JEREMIAH 17:9–10

25 God Is Bigger

"I'm here, Satan," he said. "I can't see you, and maybe you can move faster than I can, but I'm still here, and by the grace of God and the power of the Holy Spirit I intend to be a thorn in your side until one of us has had enough!"

—*This Present Darkness,* Frank E. Peretti

The Almighty has power over all things. I declare God's unlimited power in my life today!

MEDITATE ON ZECHARIAH 3:1–2

---

26 Don't Be a Lighthouse Underwater

I hadn't given one thought to the old woman in this house. The trouble with drowning in the mess of your own life is that you're not in any shape to save anyone else. You can't be a lighthouse when you're underwater yourself.

—*The Prayer Box,* Lisa Wingate

Isaiah cried out to God before doing God's work. I will ask God to restore a firm foundation in my life so I can continue to serve the Lord in strength.

MEDITATE ON ISAIAH 58:9–14

---

27 | Am Not Lost

"Jesus?" he whispered as his voice choked. "I feel so lost."
A hand reached out and squeezed his and didn't let go. "I know,
Mack. But it's not true. I am with you and I'm not lost. I'm sorry
it feels that way, but hear me clearly: **you are not lost.***"*

—*The Shack,* William Paul Young

David knew what it was like to feel lost and he cried out to
God over and over. Read the Scripture meditation aloud
today and claim the promise David claimed.

MEDITATE ON PSALM 61:1–3

---

28 It's Time to Take a Seat

Through every cloud God wants me to unlearn something.
He wants me to simplify things, to put other things and other
people aside until it is just me and Him. He doesn't want me to
do anything more, He wants me to sit at His feet and listen to
His voice. When once again He is the Father and I am the child,
our relationship is restored.

—*A Time to Mend,* Angela Elwell Hunt

Martha learned nothing was more important that sitting in
Jesus's presence. Although I may be tempted to get everything done, I choose to spend time with God above all else.

MEDITATE ON LUKE 10:38–42

---

29 Keep Coming

"There's your final piece," Sully said. He had barely enough control left to get the last words out. "Keep saying, 'Dear God, dear God.' There may still be suffering—but keep touching those people, Lucia, and He won't let you suffer alone anymore."
—*Healing Waters*, Nancy N. Rue and Stephen Arterburn

We should not ever give up coming to God. Go back to God with thanksgiving and a prayer you'd given up on.

MEDITATE ON PHILIPPIANS 4:6

---

30 Wherever I Go

"I'm afraid," she said in a small voice, small as a lone firefly in an endless field.
"I know," he said. "But fear always comes with a door, a door that leads straight through."
Abra tried to smile at him and took a deep breath, the sword trembling in her hands.
—*The Edge of Over There*, Shawn Smucker

With Jesus, there is always a way through my fear. I am strong and courageous, trusting the Lord will be with me wherever I go!

MEDITATE ON JOSHUA 1:9

---

31 In Everything, Give Thanks

"I have just four words to leave with you. Four words that have spoken volumes of truth into my life . . . **In everything, give thanks**.*"*

That was the lifeboat in any crisis. Over and over again, he had learned this, and over and over again, he had to be reminded.

"In everything, Father?"

"In everything."

—*Somewhere Safe with Somebody Good*, Jan Karon

The hard things I face never outweigh the goodness of God. I will give thanks to the Lord in everything as an act of faith that I trust God in all things.

MEDITATE ON COLOSSIANS 3:17

---

32 In the Waiting Room

"Havin' to wait gives us time to learn that He's always standing with us, teaching constant love and patience, until we finally come to the point of prayin', 'Thy will be done,'" Frannie pointed out.

Sallie nodded. "Jah . . . but the waiting is often hard."

—*The Ebb Tide*, Beverly Lewis

There is blessing in waiting; a quiet opportunity to pursue God. Do something radical today: Thank God for your waiting. Use the time of waiting to connect with Him, even when it feels hard.

MEDITATE ON LAMENTATIONS 3:25–26

---

33 Be Faithful

"I've seen him in the summer standing outside an open window, staring off into the sunset. Seems to me he's praying. Some people are given a great gift of not caring what others think or about anything but being faithful to what they're called by God to do. I think Jasper is one of those people."

—*Dogwood*, Chris Fabry

Lord, help me be faithful to whatever You call me to, regardless of anything else in my life.

MEDITATE ON MATTHEW 25:21

---

34 Answer the Call

Think about it. Pray about it. The fact that you're concerned about doing the right thing means you're halfway there. Just remember, you're not responsible for everyone else's actions. Only your own. So whatever decision you make, be sure you're doing it because it's what God would have you do, not simply because it's most comfortable.

—*The Saturday Night Supper Club*, Carla Laureano

I am willing to hear God's calling. In quiet stillness I listen for what God is calling me to do.

MEDITATE ON 1 SAMUEL 3:1–16

---

35 Talk About Jesus

After that, his faith could never be something passive, a pleasant outing to a friendly church service. Faith became everything, because heaven held one of his own. He was passionate about making sure his family all wound up together in heaven.

—*Between Sundays*, Karen Kingsbury

Jesus teaches us to proclaim the gospel to everyone. I will tell others about Jesus today!

MEDITATE ON MARK 16:15

---

36 Meet the Needs Around Me

See, that's the thing. The church at its worst is ugly. It's corrupt and self-serving and destructive. But the church at its best? It changes the world. It defends the oppressed, cares for the poor, and walks alongside those who need it most.

—*Then There Was You*, Kara Isaac

Taking care of the poor should be done willingly. I will be alert and responsive to those in need around me today.

MEDITATE ON DEUTERONOMY 15:7–11

---

37 Love Has No Agenda

All I want from you is to trust me with what little you can, and grow in loving people around you with the same love I share with you. It's not your job to change them or to convince them. You are free to love without an agenda.

> —*The Shack,* William Paul Young

True love and God's grace are the best things we can give others. Think of one way to show someone grace and love today.

MEDITATE ON 1 PETER 4:8–11

---

38 Turn and Walk Away

And let me tell you—carrying sad memories will wear you out. You've got to put them down and walk away. Do whatever you must to put emotional space between yourself and your past. That's the only way you're going to make it through.

> —*The Note,* Angela Elwell Hunt

God promises renewal as we let go of the past. Think of something from the past that you have been holding on to. Picture yourself turning and walking away from it.

MEDITATE ON ISAIAH 43:18–19

---

39 A Life of Bridges

Isabelle's green eyes sparkle with adventure, her hair tumbling about the pillow in soft spirals. She is already lost. "Fear builds walls instead of bridges. I want a life of bridges, not walls."
—The Prayer Box, Lisa Wingate

We do not need to fear when we trust in God. I declare these promises in my spirit today!

MEDITATE ON PSALM 56:3–4

---

40 A New Kind of Gift

Yet it seems to me finishing well in this life is not so much about who is the best or greatest at something, but rather who embraces lowliness of heart. Laying down one's rights—meekness—is a blessed virtue, one that must surely come straight from the Throne of Grace.
—The Prodigal, Beverly Lewis

Moses was blessed for his meekness and given great honor by God. Ask God to bless you with a meek spirit like Moses, that you may be used and blessed by God all of your days.

MEDITATE ON NUMBERS 12:3

---

41 | Walk in Deliverance

Dr. Ayers folds his hands across his slim midsection and locks eyes with mine. Though the laugh lines deepen at the corners, his gaze tells me clearly that I must not miss what he is about to say.

"He wants you to remember who delivered you from that time, Shauna. That's the point of holding on to memory: delivery, not darkness."

—*Kiss,* Ted Dekker and Erin Healy

The Almighty delivered me from the hard times in my past. I do not live in the darkness of hard seasons; I live in the delivery God brings!

MEDITATE ON GALATIANS 5:1

42 It Starts Now

Doug's voice softened. "Jeff, every day of your life you'll have to make decisions about what kind of man you want to be. It's not going to start when you're older. It starts right now. And every time you make a decision to be less than what God wants for you, you're denying yourself some of God's blessings."

—*Last Light,* Terri Blackstock

May I seek God fully that I can become all the Lord wants me to be, living in the blessing of the Almighty.

MEDITATE ON PSALM 119:9

43 Rivers Can Move Mountains

"Well, you know how a river moves a mountain." The words surprised me at first, but I knew where they were coming from. "Stone by stone," she finished.

—*The Prayer Box,* Lisa Wingate

Adam modeled the value of dedication as he cared for the Garden of Eden. I'll shift my focus from the big tasks I face to the small steps I need to take to get there.

MEDITATE ON GENESIS 2:15

44 Put It Down and Walk Away

Go straight to God, and dump it right at His feet. You go down with it if you have to. Then leave it there and go on and do what you know is right **now***. That other is done. It doesn't make you who you are. It just teaches you who to be.*

—*Healing Stones,* Nancy N. Rue and Stephen Arterburn

Like David, we are promised that God will hold our burdens and sustain us. Instead of carrying my problems, I'll leave them at the cross and walk away in freedom.

MEDITATE ON PSALM 55:22

45 Trusting God's Plans

The ship swayed to the side, and Hezzie gently drifted with it.
"And what do you want?"

Mercy let loose a heavy sigh laden with the weight of both guilt
and frustration. "Not this."

"The plans we make ain't always the ones God wants for us.
Sometimes He has something else He wants doin', and we just
have to accept that."

—*Missing Mercy,* Stephenia H. McGee

Accepting God's plans can feel hard. Lord, make me a person
who trusts in Your plans instead of my own.

MEDITATE ON JEREMIAH 29:11

---

46 God Hears, Cares, and Answers

She looked off to the mountain before returning her gaze to
him. "No matter what else you do, Yuri, please promise me
you'll pray. Seek the Lord first and foremost. He will answer
you, although it might not be the solution you expect."

—*Twilight's Serenade,* Tracie Peterson

When we bring our prayers to God, we can trust that the Lord
of all the world hears us, cares about us, and answers us.

MEDITATE ON 2 CHRONICLES 7:14

---

47 Heal Relationships with Repentance

Perhaps this is how it would always be from now on. We would be together, but not true sisters of the heart. We could tolerate one another, maybe even enjoy the other's presence for some time, but that closeness, that intimacy, might never be realized. I wondered if I could live the rest of my life like that.

Then I realized I might just have to. I could only bring my repentance to the table of our relationship. Lydia would have to bring the forgiveness.

—*Freedom's Ring,* Heidi Chiavaroli

Repentance is a gift God calls all of us to, even in our relationships with others. God will strengthen me to repent when I hurt someone in my life.

MEDITATE ON ACTS 3:19

---

48 Joy Is an Absolute Truth We Can Trust

"I've been listening to her, too, and now I'm remembering true life. And this . . . " He pointed to the mural. "Something about this is significant. It's a good thing. It somehow reminds me that joy isn't a feeling, it's a truth."

—*A Portrait of Emily Price,* Katherine Reay

We can trust that joy is an absolute truth even when we don't see it.

MEDITATE ON 1 PETER 1:8–9

---

49 One Big Puzzle

Puzzles forced me to look at something from several angles before I moved on, to look again, and again, and possibly again because each piece—no matter how small or seemingly insignificant—was critical to the whole.

—When Crickets Cry, Charles Martin

We all form one body in Christ. I thank God for the piece of the puzzle I fulfill, instead of trying to be a different piece.

MEDITATE ON 1 CORINTHIANS 12:12–27

50 When I'm at the End of Myself

Not that they were out of danger yet. There was still the matter of being found before they ran out of food to eat. He would have to trust God for that, for he was helpless to do anything about it himself. His grandfather had said that was always the best place to be. At the end of oneself was the best place to discover the Lord at work.

—A Matter of Character, Robin Lee Hatcher

At the end of ourselves, there is room for Christ to exist. As I breathe in, I am reminded of Christ living and breathing in me.

MEDITATE ON GALATIANS 2:20

51 Jesus Understands How I Feel

The nausea was back, but Kari held it at bay. **Get me through this, God, please.**

A verse came to mind, one that had comforted Kari before. It was the shortest verse in the Bible: **Jesus wept.** *If he cried over Jerusalem, if he cried over the death of Lazarus, surely he was crying now over the death of her dreams, the death of her marriage.*

—*Redemption,* Karen Kingsbury and Gary Smalley

The Almighty God knows how I feel, even when I'm at my lowest. I bring all my feelings to God, confident the Almighty will show me mercy.

MEDITATE ON ISAIAH 53:3

---

52 Where Our Greatness Lies

"Father, help these young people to see. Help them to show the world that our greatness is not in things we do for ourselves, but in things we do for others. In power that channels itself into kindness, in a hand outstretched in love."

—*The Prayer Box,* Lisa Wingate

Take a moment and think about where you focus more: on yourself or others. Ask God to show you a way to focus on others today.

MEDITATE ON PHILIPPIANS 2:4

---

53 No Longer Held Back

"Tell me what holds you back," he said.

He already knew the answer, I reckoned. He merely wanted to hear me say it. "Fear," I admitted, and then decided to open my heart to him. "Fear that I'll fail. Fear that I will not fit into the palace and make myself and my father and you into a laughingstock."

"You may fail; I cannot deny it. But if you go through life making every decision based on what is safest, you will look back one day and discover that you have missed out on the best."

—*Harvest of Rubies*, Tessa Afshar

I have nothing to fear in the Lord! I walk forward today believing in what God has for me.

MEDITATE ON LUKE 12:6–7

54 God Always Gives Love

"God has given us these five wonderful children and still I want more . . . I'm afraid the children will suspect how I feel. I can't stand the thought that they would think they're not enough. I do love them with all my heart and praise God for them every day."

"They're not going to think that. They know how you love them. Every Christian has hurts and this is one of yours, but you go to God every time and he holds you."

—*A Gathering of Memories*, Lori Wick

The Lord is good to me, full of hope and love through the Holy Spirit who is living inside me.

MEDITATE ON ROMANS 5:5

55 Faith Is a Risk Worth Taking

She looked at the steering wheel. Women were not permitted to drive in Saudi Arabia. Perhaps that was reason enough to try it. She felt a grin pull at her lips.

"You promise me it will be safe?"

"There's always risk in life's most rewarding pursuits, isn't there?"

She slid behind the wheel.

—*Blink of an Eye,* Ted Dekker

Walking in faith sometimes requires risk. I trust God to give me the courage to take risks in faith to honor the Lord and bring about the goodness of God.

MEDITATE ON JOHN 2:1–11

---

56 God's Thoughts

"Tell me what you've got planned."

"What makes you think I have plans?"

"I know you, Francie. I bet you have a notebook with all your plans written in it. You always were the little organizer. Everything had to be in order for you, everything had to make sense. I hope you've learned that some things don't make sense, no matter how hard you try to make sense of them."

—*The Amen Sisters,* Angela Benson

God understands all I do not. I trust in the Lord's ways over my own feelings and understanding.

MEDITATE ON ISAIAH 55:8

---

57 God Never Changes

"You can put your boots in the oven, but that doesn't make them biscuits."

I didn't need a translation. But then he surprised me by offering one.

"You can say whatever you want about something, but that doesn't change what it is."

—Chasing Fireflies, Charles Martin

No matter what we think or feel, God does not change. I allow myself to rest in the promise that God never changes.

MEDITATE ON MALACHI 3:6

58 I Can Depend on God

"Jennifer died. Stephen left. And the fear eats at me because I'm never sick and something is wrong."

"Jennifer's waiting for you in heaven, and Stephen will come back. Depend on God, and the fear will find its right size. He's bigger than whatever is wrong."

—The Rescuer, Dee Henderson

Declare God bigger than your problems, fears, and worries today. Trust in His power to help you overcome whatever struggles you face.

MEDITATE ON JEREMIAH 32:17

59 The Holy Assignment of Family

"You could make something of yourself if you'd try . . . "

"We don't all have to be in the limelight to be reaching our potential," Jack said, keeping his voice even. "There's something to be said for raising a family and being part of my community."

—*Lonestar Secrets,* Colleen Coble

Caring for our loved ones is an important calling and one way we show the love of God to others. Consider all you do for your family today a holy assignment.

MEDITATE ON 1 TIMOTHY 5:8

---

60 Not a Lot of Faith

"You have to get to know God on a very intimate level in order to have the kind of faith that will withstand the storms life throws at you. It's a good thing that we only have to have the amount of a mustard seed. Sometimes that's about all I can find."

—*Always Watching,* Lynette Eason

God is so good, to do so much even when our faith is tiny. Find a seed of faith and offer it to God today to see what the Lord does!

MEDITATE ON MATTHEW 17:20

---

61 Happiness Is Mine

*Brandon faced her. "Well, I guess what I **want** and what I'm stuck with are two different things."*

*Wishing she could make him feel more at ease, Hen paused a moment. Then, realizing she was staring at her wounded husband, she headed back to the kitchen. **Happiness isn't wanting what you can get, but wanting what you have**, she thought.*

—*The Judgment,* Beverly Lewis

God has given us a good life to rejoice in. I can look around and thank God for one thing I see, offering true gratitude and a smile.

MEDITATE ON ECCLESIASTES 3:9–14

62 Celebrating Life

Don't forget that in the midst of all your pain and heartache, you are surrounded by beauty, the wonder of creation, art, your music and culture, the sounds of laughter and love, of whispered hopes and celebrations, of new life and transformation, of reconciliation and forgiveness.

—*The Shack,* William Paul Young

David wrote Psalm 100 as a special psalm of thanksgiving. Read today's verses aloud and thank God for three amazing things today.

MEDITATE ON PSALM 100

63 Remember the Good

Memories are beautiful things, Boy. When the person that ya loved is gone, when the happy time is over, then ya've still got yer memories. Thank God fer this special gift of His that lets ya sorta live yer experiences again and again. S'pose there ain't no price one would settle on fer the worth of memories.

—Once Upon a Summer, Janette Oke

God gives the gift of memories, like getting through a hard season or reaching a milestone. Memories can help us grow, learn, and celebrate. Thank God for a sweet memory today.

MEDITATE ON JOHN 14:26

64 Come to God in Childlike Wonder

"I really don't. I just don't know what to do." Lydia pulled back and smiled.

"Often admitting our weakness and fear is the first step to finding rest in God. Our trust in Him isn't conveyed through superhuman confidence, as much as it comes in the way of childlike reliance on Him."

—Morning's Refrain, Tracie Peterson

God wants us to come to Him like children—full of questions, wonder, and honesty. Put aside all the formal ways you think you need to come to God and come to the Lord simply, as a child.

MEDITATE ON MATTHEW 18:1–5

65 | I Am a Water Walker

Know that you are loved, my dear . . . Know that you can and will rise above all your fears. I now call you water walker. Water Walker? Yes, you walked through the waters of your fear, didn't you?

—*Water Walker,* Ted Dekker

Even when my fears feel like an ocean, God calls me to walk in faith upon the waves. I am a water walker with Jesus.

MEDITATE ON MATTHEW 14:22–33

66 God Loves Perfectly

"God loves us perfectly. He is love, and He can heal all the hurt inside you. I can't do it. No human being can. Including you. Only one person can reach down into our messed-up souls. You don't have to believe that just because I said it. You just have to give Him a chance. Bruised, battered, scarred . . . He doesn't care. He's got the answer to all of it. Healing for everything that hurts us."

—*Fatal Frost,* Nancy Mehl

God's love is perfect for me, healing me from all things that hurt me. The Lord is the One who oversees my soul.

MEDITATE ON 1 PETER 2:24–25

67 Finding Courage

"'Courage is fear on its knees,'" quoted Ella Mae, looking again at Amelia. "And that, my dear, might just be the answer to the pickle you're in."

The truth of the saying resonated so strongly, her eyes welled up. "I'll remember this always," Amelia managed to say. "Thank you, Ella Mae."

—*The Fiddler*, Beverly Lewis

When we wait on God, He makes us strong. I don't need to have my own courage. When I go to God I will receive all the courage and strength I need.

MEDITATE ON PSALM 27:14

68 God Stays

Give me Your peace, Father . . . I need You.

The response wasn't audible. It simply was.

I am with you, daughter.

Like a constant assurance Bailey carried with her, God remained. All things might change. Love could come and go and friendships could fade. But God stayed. It was the truth that kept her company on the loneliest nights.

—*Loving*, Karen Kingsbury

Even in the lonely moments, God never leaves my side. I trust the steadfast, faithful presence of the Lord.

MEDITATE ON ZEPHANIAH 3:17

69 The Edge of the Nest

*And just as simply as that, it was over. She was no longer a
student in the local town. She was a graduate. An adult. She
thought she should feel something. Older. Wiser. But she felt
nothing but a strange emptiness. An inner knowledge that she
was now on the edge of the nest, ready to try her own wings.
That she would need to find her own place in the world.*

—*A Searching Heart,* Janette Oke

Just as God promised Samuel, God will be with us as we grow.
Ask God for boldness to try your wings and trust the Lord to
catch you.

MEDITATE ON 1 SAMUEL 3:19–21

---

70 Worry in a Straight Line

*She knew Stephen. The first hours after such a death, he
wouldn't want to talk about it. Tomorrow would be better.
"It will wait."*

*"Then if you don't mind a suggestion—plan what you will do,
and then set it aside until tomorrow," Cole said. "You tend to
worry things in circles. Try to worry in a straight line."*

—*The Healer,* Dee Henderson

I alone can't ensure all my plans will work out. But I will give
my plans to God, trusting that God will make my path straight.

MEDITATE ON PROVERBS 3:5–6

---

71 People Can Be Hard to Love

Oftentimes we reach out to people who would rather not be reached. We love people who reject our love and would just as soon spit in our face, but Jesus asks us to go on loving—go on reaching. It's easy to love someone when they love us, but so much harder to love when we are treated poorly by that person.

       —Where My Heart Belongs, Tracie Peterson

God calls us to love everyone, even people who do not treat us well. God helps me love people even when it feels hard.

MEDITATE ON LUKE 6:27–28

---

72 The One Answer

How was she going to do it? She didn't know. She had a hundred questions and just one answer. But the one answer she had trumped all the questions. That answer?
God.

       —Undeniably Yours, Becky Wade

God is all I need. The Lord is the answer to every question and circumstance in my life, fully faithful to be the same in all I face for all my days.

MEDITATE ON JOHN 11:25

---

73 The God of Old

"Our trust in Yahweh grows like trust in any other. The better we know Him, the more we can trust Him. But because He is a Being beyond our knowing, His ways will always be beyond our understanding. That's where trust and faith divide." He kissed her head and tilted her chin to capture her gaze. "Even when I can't trust Him, I can have faith in the fathomless God of Abraham, Isaac, and Jacob, whose power and promise work for the **eternal** *good of His people."*

—*Miriam,* Mesu Andrews

I can have faith in the never-changing, always loving God of Abraham, Isaac, and Jacob. Their God is my God, full of power for me!

MEDITATE ON MATTHEW 22:32

---

74 God Is Always Beside Me

When Shauna was a kindergartener, her mother taught her a ditty to say in the nights when bad dreams frightened her. How did it go? It had not come to mind for many, many years, so when Shauna found herself saying it aloud, the rhyme surprised her.

God is with me. Jesus is here. The Spirit is greater than my fear.

—*Kiss,* Ted Dekker and Erin Healy

When I am afraid, I trust that God never leaves my side. God is bigger than any fear or worry I have.

MEDITATE ON DEUTERONOMY 31:8

---

75 There Is a Plan

"And I have discovered that God had it all planned—even before I had caught on to it," Grace finished.

It was a nice story, though certainly with its share of personal sorrow. Virginia felt even more regard for Rodney's wife-to-be. She hoped they would be very happy together and counted the days until they could all share in the upcoming wedding celebration.

—A Searching Heart, Janette Oke

We can meditate and trust God's ways. Spend time reading God's Word, reminding yourself that His ways are for your good.

MEDITATE ON PSALM 119:15

---

76 It's Always a Good Time for Truth

Alan shook his head. "It's too late. Everything's ruined."

"You still have the letters." Chaplain Gray sat back in his chair, as if he'd said all there was to say.

"I told you. Ellie doesn't know about them."

"Maybe she should." He looked from the Bible back to Alan. "It's never too late with truth. It stands outside time."

—The Chance, Karen Kingsbury

God is full of truth and grace. I can tell the truth with love, confident the Lord will equip me to be honest even when it feels hard.

MEDITATE ON EPHESIANS 4:25

---

77 God Will Renew Me

He could give it over to God and trust that things would be kept in His hand. He felt completely renewed. Perhaps this was what it was all about. Leaning on God when life made no sense, as well as when the answers seemed clear.

> —*A Lady of Secret Devotion,* Tracie Peterson

I trust God to renew me today as I give my worries to the Lord. I can lean on God, even when life doesn't make sense.

MEDITATE ON 2 CORINTHIANS 4:16
---

78 It All Works Out

"Josh, I don't understand all about God, but there's one thing that I'm as sure of as the fact that I live and breathe. He loves us. He loves us completely, and always keeps our good in mind. I don't know how losin' your pup is for your good, Josh, but I **am** *sure that it can be or God wouldn't have let it happen."*

> —*Once Upon a Summer,* Janette Oke

Think of something that feels hard in your life right now and declare your belief that God will work it out for His good as He promised.

MEDITATE ON ROMANS 8:28
---

79 Change Is a Good Thing

You need to stretch a little. Comfort can be a dangerous thing. You stick around home all the time where it's safe and nothing ever changes, and before you know it, you get set in your ways and you quit learning, you quit changing, you don't grow anymore.

—*Monster,* Frank Peretti

I am a person who grows and changes as God instructs each day.

MEDITATE ON PSALM 32:8

---

80 Forgiving with God's Help

"I'd like you to know," he told Henry, "that I've forgiven him. Again and again. Once done, of course, back comes the Enemy to persecute and prosecute, and I must ante up to God and forgive yet again."

"There may be circumstances in this life," said Henry, "that God uses to keep bringing us back to him, looking for his grace."

—*Home to Holly Springs,* Jan Karon

God, give me the faith to keep forgiving those who hurt me. May I keep coming back to You each time.

MEDITATE ON MATTHEW 18:21–22

---

81 Know What's Right

"I know I've said this before, Lord, but I'm so sorry for all the stupid choices I've made. I want to start over, with your guidance. I can't afford to make mistakes now. Will you turn up the volume on your voice, and turn mine down? Will you give me that wisdom you promised if we ask?"

—*Twisted Innocence,* Terri Blackstock

I trust God to give me the wisdom I need to know what is right and make good choices in my life!

MEDITATE ON PROVERBS 2:6

---

82 Come Back and Ask

"If that's what you believe the Lord is calling you to do, then you can be confident He'll go ahead of you."
Those words would comfort me if I'd thought to ask Him first.
　　　　　—They Almost Always Come Home, Cynthia Ruchti

We have all had times when we move forward on our own, without asking God. I am grateful that God is patient with me, always ready for me to come to the throne of grace.

MEDITATE ON LUKE 11:9

---

83 Keep Talking to the Father

Their time together was too precious to squander on foolish reproofs. "I asked Papa if I could stay here with you till you come back." . . . She would stay strong. She would remember the promises of Scripture. She would hope and pray and not give way.
　　　　　—The Mistress of Tall Acre, Laura Frantz

No matter what I face, I come to the Lord for hope and strength. I will keep talking to the Father, trusting the promises of God's Word in faith.

MEDITATE ON PHILIPPIANS 1:27

---

84 Precious to God

"Whatever your story, be it good or bad, I will accept. I am not your father, who will storm and rage at you when disappointed." And the warmth in his eyes made her believe every word he spoke was true.

"You are perfectly and beautifully made," Michael continued. "You are exactly as God intended for you to be, and I love you precisely as you are."

—*The Rose of Winslow Street*, Elizabeth Camden

I am precious in the sight of God. The Lord honors me and showers me with endless love.

MEDITATE ON ISAIAH 43:4

85 When Things Change

I look at him, really look at him. Six years have changed him, changed us both. I notice for the first time that his hair is starting to thin at the top. I swallow the hard lump in my throat, as big as a duck egg; this is so bittersweet. Choosing to let a good thing go in order to make room for something better is harder than I anticipated. And scary. So very scary.

—*The Enlightenment of Bees*, Rachel Linden

Even when things feel uncertain and hard, God is watching over me, protecting me, and guiding me in perfect peace.

MEDITATE ON PSALM 91:9–11

86 Living Inside Me

"My peace, my companionship," Olivia said softly, "come from my surety that the Lord loves me. Surety that because I've asked, believing He's redeemed me, He's also forgiven me and accepts me—now, as I am. He lives inside me, walks beside me, in the form of His Holy Spirit. He holds my heart, my life. He is my heart, my life."

—*Band of Sisters*, Cathy Gohlke

My peace is in the Holy Spirit that lives in me and walks beside me. My very life is filled with the Lord.

MEDITATE ON 2 CORINTHIANS 6:16

87 When God Uses People to Love

"There's a reason the Lord's Prayer was first taught to Christ's disciples, I believe," Frannie said, stuffing a towel in her tote bag. "God loves us through other people, it seems."

—*The Ebb Tide*, Beverly Lewis

When we pray, it is a conversation between God and us. But God uses those intimate times not only for our own good, but to shape our hearts to bless others.

MEDITATE ON MATTHEW 6:9–15

88 God Loves My Family

"I think I've finally realized that I cannot be Jenny's salvation,"
Virginia continued carefully, looking into Mr. Woods' face to
see if he understood. "Only God can bring about the miracle,
the rebirth. It is my job to love her, to pray for her, and to leave
the rest to Him."

—A Searching Heart, Janette Oke

The Lord loves and cares about the people in my life. I can
trust God to take care of the people I love.

MEDITATE ON 1 JOHN 4:19

---

89 On Dry Ground

She cleared her throat. "No, my dear. I know you do not under-
stand, but there is no army, no fortress, no giant that can stand
against our God. No one. I have seen his might with my own
eyes." Her voice grew stronger with each word. "I have walked
through the bottom of the sea. On dry ground. I have watched
as he humiliated Egypt and brought the mighty Pharaoh low."

—Wings of the Wind, Connilyn Cossette

There is nothing stronger than my God! The Lord makes a way
for me when it seems impossible, and I trust in the mighty
hand of the Lord!

MEDITATE ON EXODUS 14:21–23

---

90 All Created to Be Brilliant

People marvel at the genius of Mozart because he supposedly wrote "Twinkle, Twinkle, Little Star" at the age of three and composed his first symphony at the age of twelve. And yes, of course he was a genius, but another way to look at it is that he just discovered early what it was God made him to do . . . of course he was brilliant, but that's not the point. The point is he knew, and then he got to work.

—*When Crickets Cry,* Charles Martin

We should work hard for the Lord in all that we do. I will use the gifts God gave me well and work hard.

MEDITATE ON COLOSSIANS 3:23–24

---

91 God's Strength

"It's time to leave fear behind or you'll be robbed of your destiny. You don't need confidence in yourselves or in your own power. Be strong in the Lord. When disaster seems close, don't be discouraged. God will never leave you."

—*Pearl in the Sand,* Tessa Afshar

My power will never be enough. But I can be strong in the Lord! I won't be discouraged or fearful because God is always with me!

MEDITATE ON EPHESIANS 6:10

---

92 God of the Impossible

*"I need to get you out of here," Buck said. "And I have
no idea how."*

"Have you prayed?"

"Constantly."

"The Lord will make a way somehow."

"It seems impossible right now, sir."

"Yahweh is the God of the impossible," Tsion said.

—*Rapture's Witness*, Tim LaHaye and Jerry B. Jenkins

Sometimes the things God promises seem impossible to me,
but God makes all things possible. I will trust Yahweh, God of
the impossible.

MEDITATE ON GENESIS 21:1–7

93 Where I Turn

*"I quit screaming at God a long time ago, 'cause I reckon he
knows a thing or two about hurt. When things get bad . . . when
I think I've hit bottom . . . that's where I go." He nodded toward
the Sanctuary. "And he knows—I've been there many a time.
That's what gets me from there to here . . . and to there."*

—*Chasing Fireflies*, Charles Martin

Christ knew suffering. He suffered for us to have eternal life.
Christ is where I will turn when things get bad.

MEDITATE ON 1 PETER 2:21

94 Power in God's Word

She lay down on a window seat and rolled to one side, lost in other worlds. It didn't seem to matter which story he was telling; they were all powerful.

The one he was reading now was about betrayal. Tears flooded her eyes and her heart beat heavily, but she knew it would be all right, because she knew that in the end the kind of power that was in these books would never let her down.

—White: The Great Pursuit, Ted Dekker

I trust in the power of Your Word, Lord. May I meditate on His Word in all I do.

MEDITATE ON JOSHUA 1:8

---

95 My Very Own Father

Jo took a deep breath. "It surprised me. I sat in the little chair you have in the room and read Matthew 6:6, the verse you just referred to. I began to weep without any apparent reason."

"Did you figure it out?" Renny asked.

"Oh yes. The Lord spoke to my heart that he is my Father, or as the verse says, 'thy Father.' Thy Father, my Father—not just the Father of us all, but my very, very own."

—The List, Robert Whitlow

Lord, You are my perfect Father! Thank You for loving me and caring for me as Your child!

MEDITATE ON 1 JOHN 3:1

---

96 Shift My Focus

"Getting rid of the fears is never the goal," she said. "If we fix our eyes on that, then we won't be looking at Jesus. Drawing close to the Lord is what we're seeking. God is always our first desire. So, we focus on the perfect love and faithfulness of God instead of the depth of our fear. We meditate on how big God is. How trustworthy God is. How loving and gracious God is. And slowly . . . Slowly we discover our trust growing, and our fears shrinking—all by God's gift and power. Always by God's gift and power—not by our own efforts."
—*Sensible Shoes: A Story About the Spiritual Journey*, Sharon Garlough Brown

Keeping our eyes on Jesus in the presence of fear is no easy task. Like Peter in Matthew 14:22–33, I can look to Jesus instead of the trials around me.

MEDITATE ON COLOSSIANS 3:1

---

97 Winter Never Stays

Nathan still slept, so Missie sat down beside him on the blanket and listened to the soft gurgle of the spring only a few paces away. It was good to feel alive again. She thanked God that life was not always winter, that spring always came at last—to chase away the cold and heaviness, and to release one to warmth and movement again.
—*Love's Long Journey*, Janette Oke

God defines the seasons of our lives. Take a moment to find peace in your season and have hope for the spring that's always to come.

MEDITATE ON GENESIS 8:22

---

98 God Has Plans for Me

As long as he was breathing, God's greatest task for him was not yet finished. His higher purpose in life was still unfulfilled. It was why he would attend church that Sunday. The six o'clock service, same as always.

Because God had plans for him.

—*The Chance,* Karen Kingsbury

The Lord has great purpose for my life. I trust that God will show me how to walk in that purpose all my days.

MEDITATE ON 2 TIMOTHY 1:9

99 I Have a Happy Heart

Joining hands, they bowed their heads and Sophie spoke the words her mother had taught her long ago. "We thank Thee, Lord, for happy hearts, for rain and sunny weather. We thank Thee, Lord, for this our food, and that we are together. Amen."

—*The Mistress of Tall Acre,* Laura Frantz

Give me a happy heart, Lord, no matter what my day holds. I am grateful for all that I am blessed with in this very moment.

MEDITATE ON HEBREWS 12:28–29

100 The Goodness of God

"I've pondered how much is provided for us by God's good-ness. So many sources of enjoyment, and how thankful we should be. And even if afflictions come . . . we should know that they are the hand of God." She sighed, the semblance of a smile gracing the edges of her mouth.

—*A Lasting Impression,* Tamera Alexander

God's goodness is constant, never changing. I can rely on the goodness of the Lord today in all I do.

MEDITATE ON PSALM 34:8

101 Pray Without Words

We both just stood there. I let the breeze brush against my skin, the sun release the tension in my muscles. It was as close as I had felt to God in a long time. "It's like we're praying," Celeste whispered. "Only we're not saying anything."

—*False Friends and True Strangers,* Nancy Rue

Even when we have no words to pray, the Spirit intercedes for us. Think of a time you were still and felt undeniably connected to God's presence.

ROMANS 8:26–27

102 Jesus Brings Me Healing and Hope

"God is the only one who can truly heal. In this case, it seems that He heard my prayers and used Mollie—"

"—and you—"

"—to help the process along. Look at Silver Leaf. Now look at me and tell me that you're beginning to believe that there is a God. A loving God . . . where there's God, there's hope," she said. *"And where there's hope there can be healing."*

—*A Love Like Ours,* Becky Wade

I come to Jesus with the places in my life that need healing, fully trusting the Lord to bring hope and peace to my life.

MEDITATE ON LUKE 13:11–13

103 Accepting Help

"None of us is fit to do anything. It's only with the Lord's help we get by. Life is full of setbacks, Zoe. This town was dead as a doornail, but did we give up? Just put one foot in front of the next and accept the help. Accept the help."

—*Secretly Smitten,* Colleen Coble, Kristin Billerbeck, Diann Hunt, and Denise Hunter

God is eager to help us, sometimes through other people. Asking for help does not make me weak. I can ask God and those around me for help.

MEDITATE ON JOB 6:14

104 Increased Faith

"I can't. I don't have as much faith as you do."

"Faith don't come in a bushel basket, Missy. It come one step at a time. Decide to trust Him for one little thing today, and before you know it, you find out He's so trustworthy you be putting your whole life in His hands."

—*Candle in the Darkness,* Lynn Austin

Come to God with the faith you have and, just as the apostles did, ask the Lord of all things to increase it.

MEDITATE ON LUKE 17:5

---

105 Prayer Is Full of Power

"I'd prayed about which cases we should tackle together, and this one got selected."

"I'm praying we have this case solved soon."

"We'll find the caller. As Bryce likes to say, a lot of coincidences seem to occur when you pray."

—*Unspoken,* Dee Henderson

God reveals truth and direction when we pray. I can pray in confidence that God hears me and that the conversations I have with God are powerful.

MEDITATE ON 1 JOHN 5:14–15

---

106 | I Can Talk to God Day and Night

Gus yawned and closed his eyes. He didn't like to talk much at night. That was okay. It gave Joey a reason to talk to God again, 'cause God never, ever fell asleep. He asked Jonah at the pool last time, and that's what Jonah said. God stays awake all the time. In case we need to talk to Him about something.

—*Like Dandelion Dust*, Karen Kingsbury

God is always there to listen to me, day or night, no matter what I am facing. I trust that the Lord hears me.

MEDITATE ON PSALM 66:19–20

107 | I See Light and Goodness

"God layers good over the bad. It's what he does. And the more of the bad life dishes out, the more good God dishes out too. We just get so blinded—legitimately—by what hurts that we can't see the good brightening the darkness."

—*The Space Between Words*, Michèle Phoenix

I declare the goodness of the Lord! God never gives up, continually bringing light and goodness to all things.

MEDITATE ON PSALM 66:5

108 Love Wins

Their country was home to more than a hundred thousand Jews.

Truck number seven arrived, soldiers unloading more people onto the sidewalk.

"Not in their eyes," Miss Pimentel said. "Hatred stops at nothing to destroy, but love can break through the root of evil. Grow something good instead."

"We have to do something to stop this!"

"We must fight in prayer, and we must fight together, arm in arm with those we trust."

—*Memories of Glass,* Melanie Dobson

Lord, I believe Your love conquers all things. Help me be a person who shows that love to those around me at all times.

MEDITATE ON PROVERBS 10:12

---

109 More Than Getting Through

She'd found love and fulfillment, healing, friendship, here in this unexpected place, in unexpected ways, among people and crises she wouldn't have chosen for herself. She'd watched the water carry the storm debris of her life far from shore.

—*As Waters Gone By,* Cynthia Ruchti

God not only gets us through hard times, God gives us beautiful gifts in those times. Today I will look for God's abundant blessings in the hard things I walk through.

MEDITATE ON PSALM 66:12

---

110 | Walk in Freedom

*"Just remember, forgiveness is a way of setting yourself
free of the bondage put on you by others. There is liberty to
be had in it."*

—*Dawn's Prelude,* Tracie Peterson

God sees all I am and all I do, and the Great Forgiver pardons
all in mercy. I walk in complete freedom today!

MEDITATE ON ISAIAH 55:7

111 The Friend I Can Be

*I lowered the scroll and held it to my breast. I could not imag-
ine what my friend was enduring, but her spirit seemed strong.
Over the following weeks I received other messages, each of
them affirming her fondness for me and her conviction that she
would soon sit again upon the throne.*

—*Egypt's Sister,* Angela Elwell Hunt

May I be a supportive friend who guides people to trust in
Jesus in all things. And may God provide friends who do the
same for me.

MEDITATE ON ECCLESIASTES 4:9–10

112 Showing My Faith

*She tugged on a slender chain she wore around her neck
and pulled a simple cross from beneath her uniform. "I'm a
Christian." She let the cross fall back in place. "My parents
used to say faith wasn't something you could pretend about. It
wasn't real unless it looked like faith and acted like faith."*

—*Oceans Apart,* Karen Kingsbury

The Lord longs for us to do more than just say we believe; we
need to show our faith. Father, help me live out my faith in
what I say and do.

MEDITATE ON JAMES 1:22–25

113 Ask God Questions

"How can I use something that causes me to act before I think?"
*"I have no idea . . . Why don't you take that question to God?
After all, it is He who gave you the gift in the first place. Why
not see what He has in mind?"*

—*The Innocent Libertine,* T. Davis Bunn and Isabella Bunn

There is nothing we cannot ask God. Today, bring your questions to the Lord, knowing you are heard.

MEDITATE ON PSALM 5:3

114 Answers in God's Time

In the years since, he'd retreated inside himself to a place where none of his family or friends could reach him. So his mother prayed . . . and she prayed that maybe, somehow, in time, his heart would soften and he'd find love again. Funny thing about prayers. God hears them. But you just never know if, when, or how He's going to answer them.

—My Stubborn Heart, Becky Wade

Almighty God, I come to You with all my prayers, even when I don't see the answers I long for. I trust You always to answer in Your perfect time.

MEDITATE ON 1 TIMOTHY 2:8

---

115 The Storm Around Me

The Hater took his pipe and fled into the trees. The Singer then began to sing and continued on until the Madman stood directly in his path. With love that knew no fear, the Singer caught his torment, wrapped it all in song and gave it back to him as peace.

—The Singer, Calvin Miller

Thank you, Lord, for calming the storms around me. Replace the wind and waves with Your perfect peace.

MEDITATE ON MARK 4:35–41

---

116 God Provides for Today

"The past might be challenging, and the future might be unsure. And that's okay. The present is all we're given, anyway. Right?"

He'd quoted something she'd said to him after their first kiss. "Right."

—*True to You,* Becky Wade

Just like God's provisions for the Israelites, I can trust that God provides all I need for this day. I do not need to dwell on yesterday or worry about tomorrow because God provides for me.

MEDITATE ON EXODUS 16:4–6

---

117 Fall and Get Up Again

"When you walk in your destiny, you will crash and fall more times than you can count. But the secret is to hold on to God's vision for your life—and for the lives of those He puts under your charge. No matter how many times you fall, crash, and fail, you get up. You get up and face your obstacles."

—*Harvest of Gold,* Tessa Afshar

God has a great destiny for me to walk in. No matter how many times I fail, the Almighty is there to help me up and guide me through any obstacle.

MEDITATE ON PSALM 37:24

---

118 Greater Happiness

"We should not expect to have all the blessings of life and none of its trials. It would make this world too delightful a dwelling place, and I fear we would never care to leave it . . . I have come to believe that it's only by taking some of those objects from us to which our hearts so closely cling that He endeavors . . . in His kindness, to draw us from this world to one of greater happiness."

—*A Lasting Impression,* Tamera Alexander

Lord, help me see Your loving hand in my life, drawing me to an eternity with You. May I find joy and peace greater than I've ever known.

MEDITATE ON TITUS 2:11–13

119 Music Feeds Your Soul

Music has a way of filling in the missing places. It is a gift from God above, who didn't have to provide it, but he did anyway and I half think he decided life just wouldn't be as good without it . . . if you have music, there is something to feed your soul.

—*Almost Heaven,* Chris Fabry

I am thankful for the gift of music in my life. Today, God, I will honor You as songs of praise fill my soul.

MEDITATE ON EPHESIANS 5:19–20

120 Make Time for the Sunset

She was still in the midst of a phone marathon, working on a speech on fiscal policy. She needed someone to remind her to slow down. When she hung up the phone and before she could dial again, he leaned over the back of the couch and set his hands down on her shoulders. "Slip away and come watch the sunset."

She leaned her back to look at him. "There are more calls to finish."

"Those will wait. The sunset won't."

—*The Guardian,* Dee Henderson

Life is filled with little things God created that are beautiful and fleeting. I will make time today to appreciate the amazing sun.

MEDITATE ON ECCLESIASTES 9:9

121 Know God

Father, sometimes in the situations we find ourselves, it's difficult to know what to say to you. Sometimes we're unhappy. Sometimes we're distraught. Sometimes we have no idea where to turn. The world seems in such chaos. However, we know we can thank you for who you are. We thank you that you're a good God. That you care about and love us.

—*Nicolae,* Tim LaHaye and Jerry B. Jenkins

We don't have to understand everything that happens around us. We need only understand who God is and that He loves us.

MEDITATE ON PSALM 18:30

122 When Fear Barges In

Brian blinked. He had ordered himself never to think such things. Nothing could be gained by worrying and dreading the future, borrowing tomorrow's pain for today. Still, there were times when fear didn't bother knocking. Times when it kicked in the door and trampled right in. Times like these.

—*Gideon's Gift,* Karen Kingsbury

Sometimes fear barges in, whether we like it or not. I bring my fear to God, trusting my future is secure.

MEDITATE ON MATTHEW 6:33–34

123 A Complete Rebirth

For most who had gone through what she had, there'd be no healing, no freedom. But Bailey had found the answer. She'd found Jesus and, in Him, redemption and rebirth. It was time she started embracing the life He had for her, rather than drowning in regret over the sins of her past. Sins Jesus had already nailed to the cross.

—*Submerged,* Dani Pettrey

Lord, forgive me for taking on things You have already forgiven. I trust Your complete redemption and rebirth in my life!

MEDITATE ON EPHESIANS 1:7

124 It All Comes from God

"You may have been born a king's son," I frequently reminded him, "but your mother is a soldier's daughter and your father was once a shepherd. Adonai promotes some people, while He keeps others humble, and we have little choice in the matter. Never forget that everything you have, even the breath in your body, comes from the Almighty One, so be grateful for all you are given."

—Bathsheba, Angela Elwell Hunt

My life is a gift from God, the Creator of all things. I choose to be grateful for my life today!

MEDITATE ON JOB 33:4

125 Trust Brings Joy

This joy was a deep abiding peace, an assurance that God was sovereign. They didn't have to like what was happening. They merely had to trust that God knew what he was doing.

—Nicolae, Tim LaHaye and Jerry B. Jenkins

Our joy and peace do not depend on what we see or feel. We can have joy in trusting that God knows all and is in complete control.

MEDITATE ON EXODUS 3:7–8

126 Forgive Without Limits

"When a man repents of his sins, God will forgive him and welcome him back. The Lord's capacity to forgive a person who is truly repentant is without limit, without qualification. We must learn to forgive Bane, as well."

—*The Lady of Bolton Hill*, Elizabeth Camden

God is faithful to forgive me of all my sins without any qualifications. I will learn to forgive myself and others the same way.

MEDITATE ON 1 JOHN 1:9

---

127 I Am Amazed

Being near God's creation reminded her of His sovereignty and majesty. Setting the moon in the sky to control the tides . . . it awed her. Jesus walking on water, calming the storm . . . Knowing He tamed something so wild and free settled her soul in a way nothing else did.

—*The Killing Tide*, Dani Pettrey

Thank you, Creator of all things. I am in awe of all You have done and all You continue to do. Your works are amazing!

MEDITATE ON GENESIS 1:1–31

---

128 Trust the One in Control

"You want to help everybody and fix everything. But Timothy, you just can't."

"I've never been able to swallow that down."

"Remember the sign I have over my drawing board at home? 'Don't feel totally, personally, irrevocably responsible for everything. That's my job. Signed, God.'"

—*A New Song*, Jan Karon

God rules over the whole world, from the smallest thing to the heavens themselves. I can trust that God is in control.

MEDITATE ON PSALM 22:28

---

129 The Lord Stands by Me

"I wish I were as close to the Lord as you are."

"You could be."

"Maybe one day," I said, without a grain of hope.

Ethan rubbed a finger against his temple. "God is mindful of your sufferings, Elianna. He knows every tear you shed. He has not abandoned you. You must try not to abandon him."

—*Land of Silence*, Tessa Afshar

The Lord knows my suffering. God has seen every tear and still shows me love and grace. I stand by the Lord as the Lord stands by me.

MEDITATE ON PSALM 56:8

---

130 God Is Always Working

"You remember to trust in Heavenly Father. Life is blessing, but it is also testing. Take the one as you do the other and trust Him who allows all. Trust what Creator is doing, though we cannot understand it or see the full path. Honor your father."

—*A Flight of Arrows*, Lori Benton

God is always at work on my behalf. The Creator does what is best for me, giving me blessings along the way.

MEDITATE ON JOHN 5:17

---

131 God's Infinite Plan

I've never been one to mourn the passing of what could have been a promising relationship . . . Not that I think I'm more special than anyone else, mind you. But if a thing is not meant to be, I figure it's not part of God's infinite plan.

—*The Velvet Shadow*, Angela Elwell Hunt

When I feel loss or grief, the Lord still knows and plans all things. I trust God's infinite plan for my life always.

MEDITATE ON ISAIAH 46:9–10

---

132 Created to Be

It must seem like the world is ending, but wait and see what
God will do. He must have something wonderful in mind . . .
The leap of faith I took to come here showed me who He cre-
ated me to be.

—*Love Starts with Elle,* Rachel Hauck

God wants good for me, all the days of my life. I rejoice knowing the Lord will always take care of me!

MEDITATE ON LUKE 1:49

---

133 Seeing Deeper

Her father understood what had gone unsaid. "My child, never
judge a man because of his race. Never. God looks at the heart.
So should we. We are all made in God's image. Whatever reason
Mr. Chandler doesn't go to church, we'll pray we can overcome
it so that he will join us soon."

—*Wagered Heart,* Robin Lee Hatcher

Lord, help me look beyond what I see with my eyes to see
people's hearts the way You do.

MEDITATE ON 1 SAMUEL 16:7

---

134 Share Faith in Grace and Love

*"I'm honestly not even certain there **is** a God. And if there is . . .
well, I've never seen any evidence."*

*Gwen didn't look offended. Her smile remained in place as
she stood and angled toward the door. "God is real, my friend.
And I daresay you **have** seen Him—you just don't know it." She
moved to the door, then paused with her hand on the latch. "I
hope you don't mind if I pray for you."*

—*A Song Unheard,* Roseanna M. White

I am grateful that God is real in my life. I will show others hope
by speaking truth and praying for them.

MEDITATE ON 1 PETER 3:15–16

---

135 Time to Listen

*Kaaren continued rocking, letting other verses she had memo-
rized through the years bathe her mind in their healing power.
God had not turned a deaf ear. He had been waiting for her to
listen, as He always did.*

—*A Land to Call Home,* Lauraine Snelling

God longs for me to listen. May I always be willing to talk to
God, but also make time to listen to the Holy Spirit.

MEDITATE ON EZEKIEL 3:10

---

136 Having Faith When I Can't Feel God

"Are you there, Lord? Sometimes I can't sense Your Presence, I have to go on faith alone. You want us to walk by faith, You tell us so . . . don't we go on faith that the sun will set, the moon will rise, our breath will come in and go out again, our hearts will beat? Give me faith, Lord, to know Your Presence as surely as I know the beating of my own heart."

—*In This Mountain*, Jan Karon

Even in times when I struggle to sense God's Presence, I choose to walk in faith that the Lord is with me!

MEDITATE ON HEBREWS 11:1

137 Using My Gifts for God

There was Fern, standing against the doorjamb in her usual way, arms crossed against her chest. "My father had a saying: 'Burying your talents is a grave mistake.'"

Julia looked down at Menno's quilt in her lap.

Fern walked up to Julia. " . . . God has given you a good gift and you have an opportunity to give God back a gift. But not if you bury it."

—*The Keeper*, Suzanne Woods Fisher

The Lord has given me good gifts and I will not hide them. I use my gifts for the glory of God!

MEDITATE ON MATTHEW 25:14–30

138 Start Sharing Today

Wouldn't one think that the forgiven would be the quick-est to forgive others? That the redeemed would fall over one another in their rush to carry the song of deliverance to those who had yet to hear its calming melody? That those who had found refuge would do everything in their power to light the way for others?

—*When the Morning Glory Blooms,* Cynthia Ruchti

I can be bold and tell others about the good things the Lord has done for me. I will share God's love, forgiveness, and sal-vation with someone today!

MEDITATE ON MARK 16:20

139 Pray in Power

"Please." Angie's heart rate picked up speed. "If we had a number . . . or an address."

"I've told you what I know." Ember looked over her shoul-der and then back at them. "Battles are won and lost through prayer."

Angie still couldn't believe this strange conversation. Was she dreaming?

—*Angels Walking,* Karen Kingsbury

Prayer is powerful. I will pray in full expectation that God hears me and will answer me. My prayers are a weapon I can use to battle for my faith.

MEDITATE ON EPHESIANS 6:18

140 Faith that Grows

*"That's why we struggle. Until we can pray, '**Thy** will be done in earth, as it is in **heaven**,' we gonna have a whole lot of sleepless nights. We want to make our own plans and then pray, '**My** will be done, if you please Massa Jesus, in earth, as it is in **my** plans.' You got to put your life in Jesus' hands. Trust that in the end, whatever happens, He still in control."*

—*Candle in the Darkness*, Lynn Austin

My life is secure in God's hands. I can start with one step of faith and trust God to build a faith in me that will flourish.

MEDITATE ON 1 TIMOTHY 6:12

141 God Can Handle Your Worst

She'd been a fair-weather Christian before the last eighteen months. But in the recent black days, she'd touched bottom, and God was still there. Still bigger than the problems. She hit Him with her anger, her pain, and He'd taken it in and not reflected it back. Cassie was clinging to that peace she had found. Life was tough, but God was tougher.

—*The Protector*, Dee Henderson

We can take every thought, feeling, and action to God, trusting it will be shaped to glorify the Lord. I will not hold back my feelings from God. Instead, I bring them boldly to the Lord.

MEDITATE ON 2 CORINTHIANS 10:5

142 The Source of Joy

"Avraham is a grown man . . . "

"But weren't your holidays sad without him?"

"Yes, at first. But Miriam said we must learn to celebrate the true meaning of the holiday, with gratitude. She said that happiness is something that comes from our own hearts, not from other people."

—*While We're Far Apart,* Lynn Austin

I want my happiness and joy to come from the Lord. I choose to look to the King to fill my heart with joy today!

MEDITATE ON PSALM 34:5

143 Longing for God

"El-Shaddai holds my heart, Bithiah. He's the One I adore. I feel His presence when I sing."

"Oh, Miriam." Disheartened, Bithiah ached at the girl's loneliness. "A god could never fill the longing for your one true love."

"No Bithiah. A man can never fill my longing for my one true God."

—*The Pharaoh's Daughter,* Mesu Andrews

My deepest longing is filled only by God. There are no substitutes, no other things that can fill me so completely with love.

MEDITATE ON PSALM 103:1–5

144 My Father's Love

*"I like to think God carries around our pictures in His wallet
and shows them to the angels every so often. 'Why look at my
Lizzie,' He says to them. 'Isn't she the most wonderful daughter
any father could ever have?'"*

I shook my head. "I doubt that's what He'd say about me."

*Cora stood to her feet. "And that's where the problem is, isn't
it?" she asked softly. "If you don't mind, I'm gonna pray that
one of these days you'll understand how powerful the love of a
good Father really is."*

—*Inescapable*, Nancy Mehl

The Father loves me and delights in me! I am a child of the
Living God and I am loved forever!

MEDITATE ON 2 CORINTHIANS 6:18

145 Joy in My Purpose

*One thing I've learned from you and Bree is that every day is
a gift. What we do with it is our choice. For too many years
I've been throwing my days away on frivolous things, things
I thought would make me happy. But they didn't. Finding
Frannie—**that** made me more than happy. Satisfied, content,
joyous. I had a purpose.*

—*Silent Night: A Rock Harbor Christmas Novella*, Colleen Coble

I can trust in the purpose God has for me. The Lord will equip
me and fill me with joy as I step forward in my purpose.

MEDITATE ON ROMANS 9:17

146 Work with God

"Maggie came down here to work for God, but that's not what He's wanting her to do."

"It isn't? I thought we're all supposed to work for God."

"He wants us to work with Him, honey. Not for Him."

—Wonderland Creek, Lynn Austin

I never have to work on anything alone because God is always with me, at my right hand, helping me.

MEDITATE ON ISAIAH 41:13

147 God Receives Me

In the light of Miss Alice's story, I understood that the reason we have to accept other people is simply because God receives us just the way we are. Yes, all of us to the last person.

—Christy, Catherine Marshall

I can come to Jehovah just as I am. The Lord not only accepts and receives me, but loves me completely! Lord, show me how to accept others completely.

MEDITATE ON ROMANS 5:6–8

148 Compassion for the Lowest

"For shame, children." She narrowed her brows at them. "Lucy is a blessing. She's the lifeblood of your brother. If not for her, Thomas wouldn't survive."

Betsy dropped the hold on her nose, and her smile faded. Johnny watched her and then imitated.

"Moreover, Jesus showed love to the lowest, poorest, sickest people. As His followers, He calls us to do the same."

—*The Preacher's Bride,* Jody Hedlund

Lord, help me show love, compassion, and kindness to everyone around me, especially the lowest, poorest, and sickest of people, just as You did.

MEDITATE ON LUKE 14:12–14

149 God Gives Me a Way Out

"I guess I felt cornered . . . what if I can't stop?"

John slid his way closer to Kade and hugged him. "You'll stop buddy. God'll give you the strength." He thought of Charlene again. "He can give you the strength to walk away from anything bad, no matter how trapped you feel."

—*A Time to Embrace,* Karen Kingsbury

God gives us a way out of every temptation. I bring my temptation to God and ask for a way out.

MEDITATE ON 1 CORINTHIANS 10:13

150 Beauty Within

"There is nothing you can't do when you leave here. There is no taint that can't be overcome. You are a child of God, and that means that there is great, shining beauty within you."

Rosina flushed and dipped her head. "When a fine lady like you says that, I can almost believe it."

Clara smiled, and this time her smile was real. "I've believed in you all along, Rosina."

—*The Lady of Bolton Hill,* Elizabeth Camden

Rest in the promise of who you are today: I am a child of God with great, shining beauty within me!

MEDITATE ON JOHN 1:12–13

---

151 The Beginning of Belief

I put my head down and wept. "I find that so hard to believe." I felt helpless, as if everything that had ever mattered to me was passing through my fingers.

"Life is not only made up of what you can see. This is the beginning of belief."

—*The Day the Angels Fell,* Shawn Smucker

Even when it is hard to believe, we can declare our desire to believe and ask God to help our unbelief. The Lord is faithful to help me believe!

MEDITATE ON MARK 9:24

---

152 God Is Real

"Look at us here," he gestures to the hollow room. "We are openly discussing God in a place that not so long ago killed many of my friends for similar conversations. God cannot be suppressed under the evil of man. The world is harsh and cruel and full of pain. But God is real. The Holy Spirit and Mary and the saints—they're real. To believe is to trust, and when you trust, your life has meaning and purpose outside of the mere endurance of hardship."

—*Like a River from Its Course,* Kelli Stuart

The Word of God is at work in my life! I have faith that the Lord is real within me and all around me.

MEDITATE ON 1 THESSALONIANS 2:13

153 I am Not a Lone Ranger

We can't be lone rangers. You need to be fed, Hannah—not just in the sacred journey group or in your private devotions. You need other believers around you, worshiping with you and encouraging you. The very thing you've been avoiding is exactly what you need. Even if it's a struggle—even if it makes you feel lost and uncomfortable.

—*Sensible Shoes: A Story About the Spiritual Journey,* Sharon Garlough Brown

We are encouraged to live in community with believers. I will take time with other believers of Christ.

MEDITATE ON HEBREWS 10:24–25

154 Love Gives

"Sometimes the most courageous thing a man can do is run back across the battlefield and rescue the wounded." He shook his head and spat. "But don't fool yourself. It ain't glamorous. Ain't at all. It's simply a choice."

—Thunder and Rain, Charles Martin

Lord, help me be willing to sacrifice when necessary to show someone else Your holy love. I will do so with a joyful heart, grateful to love one of Your children.

MEDITATE ON EPHESIANS 5:2

155 I Believe the Good

"It's all up to you, Josh. Whenever something comes into our life that hurts us, we do the decidin'—do I let this work for my good, as God intended, or do I let bitterness grow like a bother- some canker sore in my soul?

. . . God loves you. He can help you with the hurt if you ask Him to."

—Once Upon a Summer, Janette Oke

God works all things for my good. I choose to believe the Almighty loves me and will help me see the good in whatever I walk through.

MEDITATE ON DEUTERONOMY 7:9

156 The Light Wins

Corin stumbled over to the couch and slumped down beside her. "Did you delete it?"

"I get the feeling it's not mine to delete."

"I suppose not." Corin leaned his head back again and clicked his teeth together as if he could bite the emotions coursing through his soul in two and make them die.

"You need to let some light into whatever dark closet you're hanging out in at the moment."

—*The Chair*, James L. Rubart

There is no darkness I face that can overcome the Light. The Light always wins!

MEDITATE ON JOHN 1:5

---

157 Peace for My Heart

Sometimes it is necessary to celebrate life, despite being faced with defeat and death. We have no idea what our future holds, or where we will all be next week, next month, or next year. But today, we are together; therefore, we should fellowship in peace.

—*The Alliance*, Jolina Petersheim

The future is outside my control, but God lives in me and promises peace for my heart! I can enjoy this day and fellowship with those around me in the peace of God.

MEDITATE ON ROMANS 5:1

---

158 Living for Jesus

"You're a fool, Omar. A pathetic, sissy—"

"Don't call me that!" Omar drew a gun from his belt and pointed it at Levi. "I'm sorry so many died, but I fit in here. And we all know that was never going to happen in Glenrock."

Destroying an entire village to fit in? "Just make sure that the thing you're living for is worth dying for, Omar."

—*Captives*, Jill Williamson

I choose to live for Jesus, the One who died for me.

MEDITATE ON LUKE 9:23

---

159 Jesus Had Twelve Followers

"Country music, Grandpa. That's as big as it gets. People will see my faith and they'll want Jesus. They will."

His grandfather stayed quiet, his eyes never leaving Zack's. "God doesn't measure big the way people measure big. Jesus had just twelve followers." He blinked a few times. "Fame is a demanding mistress."

—*Fifteen Minutes*, Karen Kingsbury

God's best for us may look different than we imagine, and certainly different than what the world says we should aspire to. I will trust God's best for my life.

MEDITATE ON GALATIANS 1:10

---

160 More Than Enough

*"We look at our own problems, and we say . . . why? Maybe we should look at our **blessings** and ask the same thing."*

She took a sip of her coffee. "I think I need to remember that, too. I do have enough . . . this is enough. More than enough."

—*It Had to Be You,* Susan May Warren

I can trust that God has given me good things, more than what I need. I choose to be thankful for God's blessings today!

MEDITATE ON 2 CORINTHIANS 9:8

---

161 He Is Always Good

"God is good. It'll happen," they had told her.

As if God's goodness depended upon whether or not He answered prayers the way people wanted Him to answer. The hard truth was that sometimes He didn't. He hadn't rescued Marilyn from her infertility, and He hadn't rescued Sara from her blindness. But that didn't negate His goodness. It just meant He had different plans.

—*A Broken Kind of Beautiful,* Katie Ganshert

The Lord is faithful in the goodness shown to us. May I trust in the goodness of the Lord.

MEDITATE ON PHILIPPIANS 1:6

162 A Committed Friend

Youth today didn't understand a world before social media and mobile phones, before one could search the internet for a missing person or post their picture on screens around the world. And many people—today and from years past—didn't understand or honor faithfulness. A deep commitment to those you loved, to persevere no matter what. One didn't just forget a lost friend.

—*Catching the Wind,* Melanie Dobson

May I love those in my life and be fully committed to them, persevering in Christ's strength through all things.

MEDITATE ON 2 KINGS 2:1–6

163 Transforming Me

She narrowed her eyes. "How did you know?"

"Because God doesn't promise the way will be easy—far from it—but He promises to carry us through, to give us the courage and grace we need when we need it. He most often doesn't change the circumstances; He changes us."

—*Silenced,* Dani Pettrey

Lord, transform me. Give me grace and courage to face all You give me, and help me lean on You every step of the way.

MEDITATE ON 2 CORINTHIANS 3:18

---

164 My Responsibility

"Faith is moving ahead in obedience, dear. Just moving ahead one step at a time, trusting Him, until He shows you what's next. He'll make it clear to you eventually. Sure as anything . . . Just wait on Him and then do what He says. That's truly your only responsibility. He'll take care of everything else."

—*Undeniably Yours,* Becky Wade

I choose to wait on the Lord. Even when I don't understand. Even when it feels hard. I can wait on God, full of faith in all that is promised to me.

MEDITATE ON PSALM 33:20–22

---

165 For the Glory of God

"Was it like that when you came to America?" I ask, twisting off the bottle cap and taking a long swallow of water.

Abel tips his head, a tacit agreement. "When I finally stepped onto American soil, I kissed the ground, right there at the airport arrivals curb. I thought I could leave all the sorrow behind me, all the things I had seen." He is watching the newly arrived family, but his tone of voice tells me he is far away. "But we cannot escape our experiences."

—*The Enlightenment of Bees*, Rachel Linden

God is glorified above all else. All that I am, past, present and future, is for the glory of the Lord.

MEDITATE ON ROMANS 11:36

166 When I Feel Weak

"You are forgiven a hundred times over, child."

My throat grew tight at the absolution. It seemed this woman could read my very heart, and still she loved me. I clung tighter to her hand.

She squeezed back. "Just remember: do not be frightened of the truth or of your past. The Lord can work powerfully through it."

I nodded acknowledgment. Perhaps I didn't doubt that God could work; rather I assumed He wouldn't choose to employ a cursed, weak individual like myself.

—*Freedom's Ring*, Heidi Chiavaroli

God delights in using our weakness to glorify the Almighty. I can thank God for my weakness and ask to be made strong in those places.

MEDITATE ON 1 CORINTHIANS 1:26–29

167 God in Me

". . . I'm learning that this life isn't about me anyway nor is it about what I want out of it. Following Christ is about surrender and faith and about God working through me instead of me working for God."

"Rosalie knew what it was like to surrender her life." Camden took another deep breath. "And so did my grandfather."

—*Refuge on Crescent Hill*, Melanie Dobson

Working for God will never give me the life I long for. I choose to surrender and have faith that God is working in me.

MEDITATE ON PHILIPPIANS 2:12–13

---

168 My Forgiveness Is Forever

He reached for her hand, and she allowed him to cradle it. "You are a strong and beautiful woman, Dinah," he said. "The journey ahead of us is harsh. Both the mountains we'll travel and the people you'll meet can be dangerous and unforgiving." He gave an almost imperceptible squeeze of her hand. "But neither the mountains nor the people can rob you of the forgiveness God has given—unless you let them."

—*Love Amid the Ashes*, Mesu Andrews

I am confident in the forgiveness given to me through Jesus Christ. Nothing can take that forgiveness away from me.

MEDITATE ON ACTS 13:38–39

---

169 Know Who Is in Control

In the end, this is what I have decided about my family, about the place I've come from, with all its beauty and tragedy. Yes, I can put my hands and my feet and my heart to work trying to remedy the things that are within my power, but so much of it isn't. What can't be understood and neatly sewn up must simply be let go, not in the way of giving up, but in the way of understanding who is really in control of it.

—*The Story Keeper*, Lisa Wingate

God's way always prevails. Think of something you need to let go of and give it to God.

MEDITATE ON PROVERBS 19:21

---

170 Don't Worry About the Thorns; Enjoy the Rose

He picked up one of Lorna's roses and set it in my lap. "Here." I picked it up and smelled it.

He poked me in the shoulder. "See what I mean? Thorns don't stop you from sniffing. Or putting them in a vase on the kitchen table. You work around them." He stuck a finger in the air. "Why? 'Cause the rose is worth it." He looked at me. "Think what you'd miss."

—*Chasing Fireflies*, Charles Martin

1 Thessalonians calls us to rejoice and give thanks in all circumstances. Lord, give me a heart full of gratitude and rejoicing.

MEDITATE ON 1 THESSALONIANS 5:16–18

---

171 My Heart Is Content

She looked up at the big house, at the white clapboard siding and the green shutters with little cut-out pine trees, at the stone foundation the house rested on. It was fancier than the simple Amish farmhouses she was used to. A pretty house, to be sure, but would it ever be a home to her? Would she ever learn to be content in this life she chose? She felt so strange inside. Sad and lonely and missing the life she thought she would have.
—*The Choice,* Suzanne Woods Fisher

Lord, make my heart content with all You give me. I want to choose You, Your hope, Your truth, Your love over all things.

MEDITATE ON 1 TIMOTHY 6:6–7

172 Do Not Fear Change

"I'm so tired of this war," Mary went on. "You know that the papers are full of dire news about Lincoln's chances of getting reelected. Some are calling for him to rescind emancipation to get enough votes. What will happen to all who have escaped north should the worst transpire? What would happen to you?"

"Worrying won't change things," he said. "Change happens when the cost of keeping things the way they are is too high."
—*We Hope for Better Things,* Erin Bartels

Worry and fear will not consume me. I stand on the promises of God to be with me in all things, an ever-present help in all trouble.

MEDITATE ON PSALM 46:2–3

173 I Walk in Freedom and Grace

"Shame is a hold that sin uses on you. As long as you're ashamed of the sin, it has a hold on you. When you can name it, and walk away from it, you're walking in the power of God. That's what the Lord wants from His people. Sin and shame have no place in the life of a man or woman of God."

—The Amen Sisters, Angela Benson

My sin does not keep me from God. I accept God's forgiveness and walk forward without shame.

MEDITATE ON JOHN 8:1–11

---

174 Living in the Promise

Michael had once read to her how God had cast a man and woman out of Paradise. Yet, for all of their human faults and failures, God had shown them the way back in.

—Redeeming Love, Francine Rivers

Although sin is part of life, God does not leave us in that place. God has promised a place in Paradise for me! I can live in Revelation's promise!

MEDITATE ON 1 PETER 1:3–4

---

175 Patient Prayer

After putting on my pajamas, I took my Bible and journal downstairs to the front room. I turned on a small lamp and knelt in front of the sofa. God could speak quickly, or he might make me wait. To set a timetable for an answer would be disrespectful to his sovereignty. God was merciful, but prayer wasn't always meant to be a desperation plea by someone wanting a quick fix to a thorny problem.

—*Deeper Water,* Robert Whitlow

I will wait on God to reveal the answers to my prayers at just the right time. I wait on the Lord full of hope and faithful anticipation.

MEDITATE ON PSALM 130:5

176 Enjoy Time

What had the guy said? **Someday when you're old and gray like us, you'll look back on that picture and understand about the passing of time. Don't blink, young people. Enjoy every minute.**

—*Ever After,* Karen Kingsbury

God gives us each day as a gift to enjoy. Instead of rushing through my days, I will try to enjoy them and thank God for each one.

MEDITATE ON PSALM 90:12

177 Just Keep Going

She had spent a long time sitting in the rose garden behind her home that night, looking at the stars, talking to God, trying to figure out what she should do.

She wasn't a coward. If she were, years before she would have retreated back into her shell and pulled back entirely from life. She was a fighter. Life knocked her down, and she coped by getting up and moving on.

—*Danger in the Shadows,* Dee Henderson

No matter what we face, God equips us to keep moving forward with strength from the Lord. Move forward today, grateful for God's strength to keep going.

MEDITATE ON PHILIPPIANS 3:12

178 Unending Grace

"Listen carefully, Elisabeth. Your mother finally realized what grace was all about. It means we don't have to please God, because we can't."

Elisabeth was confused. "You mean we're not supposed to try to—"

He cupped her face in his hands. "We try to live godly lives to show our thanks to him for grace."

—*Though None Go with Me,* Jerry B. Jenkins

My life is a reflection of God's grace. All I am and all I do show gratitude to the Lord for the mercy given to me.

MEDITATE ON 2 CORINTHIANS 2:8–9

179 When I Don't Understand

"That's all I'm doing, choosing to trust Jesus even if I don't understand what or why something is happening. Jesus wants you to choose to trust Him again. He won't take that trust you place in Him lightly."

—The Guardian, Dee Henderson

Trusting Jesus is a choice, and it can feel challenging when our circumstances or the things around us don't make sense. I choose to trust God even when I don't understand, and God will bless me.

MEDITATE ON JEREMIAH 17:7–8

---

180 The Hope I Long For

Deborah shook her head. "I've searched deep inside myself and found that place empty."

"Oh, darling, your hope doesn't come from within—not in the sense of self, anyway. It comes from God alone. If not, then it will crumble and blow as dust to the wind. You have only to fix your sights on Jesus."

—Hearts Aglow, Tracie Peterson

It is freeing to remember our hope isn't something we are responsible for on our own. I trust God to be the hope my soul longs for.

MEDITATE ON PSALM 42:5

---

181 Time to Stop Talking

"Prayer isn't just about asking for things. It's taking time to hear what God is saying, too, just like any good conversation. Once we finally stop talking and demanding and begging for things, it's easier to hear what God is trying to say to us. Give it a chance, Josephine."

—*All Things New*, Lynn Austin

God promises us the ability to hear all the Lord has for us. Instead of talking to God today, try listening for the Voice of God.

MEDITATE ON REVELATION 3:20

182 I Can Rest in the Father's Hand

As his breathing became rhythmic and deep, his last conscious thought was different from what it had been for so long. Rather than the dread fear that came with life as an international fugitive, he rested in the knowledge that he was a child of the King, a saved, forgiven, precious, beloved son safe in the hollow of his Father's hand.

—*The Indwelling: The Beast Takes Possession*, Tim LaHaye and Jerry B. Jenkins

No matter what I've done or what I am hiding from, God sees me, knows me, and loves me.

MEDITATE ON JOHN 10:28

183 God Wants Me to Be Myself

"Sometimes you have to gag on fancy before you can appreciate plain, th' way I see it. For too many years, I ate fancy, I dressed fancy, I talked fancy. A while back, I decided to start talkin' th' way I was raised t' talk, and for th' first time in forty years, I can understand what I'm sayin'."

—At Home in Mitford, Jan Karon

God created me and knows me. I am fully equipped to do God's work just as I am.

MEDITATE ON EPHESIANS 2:10

---

184 Everything I Wanted

In her secret heart, she hid a sadness over her childless state. She was very fond of her pupils, and of Alice, in particular. But it wasn't the same as having a child of her own, as being someone's mamma.

God was good, she did not doubt. But that did not always mean He gave you everything you wanted.

—The Ladies of Ivy Cottage, Julie Klassen

I trust that God knows all my needs, and that the Great Provider will give me all that is best for me.

MEDITATE ON MATTHEW 6:8

---

185 All Grace and Love

Her lip quivered. "But I am so unworthy."

"We all are. That's the beauty of God's grace and the depth of Christ's love. "God loves you . . . And so do I."

—Submerged, Dani Pettrey

Christ makes me worthy. I am given grace and loved fully, forever.

MEDITATE ON JOHN 3:16–17

---

186 Let Peace Rule

Deep down in the part of her soul she could not see, peace ruled. Since the day she'd cried in church for two hours and surrendered herself to the One who truly, unconditionally loved and defended her, a new hope was born.

Jesus would heal her past and take care of her todays and her tomorrows. Her good Father held her future in His hands.

—The Love Letter, Rachel Hauck

God will lift the baggage I carry from the past; He is with me today and my future is secure. I can rest in gratitude for all the Lord is doing for me!

MEDITATE ON LUKE 12:32

---

187 God Is Still Good

"Thank you for that—for respecting Becky's confidences. You gave an interview when your daughter was still missing. You were asked the question: 'What has this done to your faith?' You answered along the lines of, 'God is good, and I love Him. Right now, God is permitting a very hard thing. Why, I don't know, but I still trust Him.'"

—*Taken*, Dee Henderson

We all face hard—sometimes incredibly hard—things. But I can declare these truths: God is still good and I still love the Lord.

MEDITATE ON 2 CORINTHIANS 4:17

---

188 God Shows How to Love

He fell silent, deep in thought. "I do love her, but . . . it terrifies me. I don't want to love her only to lose her again."

"Yuri, love isn't about living in fear. It's not about controlling the hearts of those around you. It is patient and kind. It endures and believes the very best. It never gives up. Just as Britta has never given up hoping that you would love her."

—*Twilight's Serenade*, Tracie Peterson

It is not my job to control others. It is only my job to love well, the way God shows me how to love.

MEDITATE ON 1 CORINTHIANS 13:4–7

---

189 Jesus Never Disappoints

"Well, I'm going to church. But I've got to tell you that it's full of hypocrites."

Father Tim laughed. If there was ever a popular refrain in modern Christendom, that might be it.

"My friend, if you keep your eyes on Christians, you will be disappointed every day of your life. Your hope is to keep your eyes on Christ."

—At Home in Mitford, Jan Karon

In our lives, people are a gift to help point us to Jesus. But they are human. I choose to keep my eyes on Christ rather than people.

MEDITATE ON ISAIAH 26:3

---

190 Taking One Step at a Time

"Have faith that God has you right where you need to be, though all around seems bewildering. Have faith that He sent you help when you needed it, that He will guide you on from this moment too. One step at a time. You don't have to figure it all out now."

—The Pursuit of Tamsen Littlejohn, Lori Benton

My salvation and refuge are in God alone. There is nothing I need to fear in the future because the Lord is in complete control of my steps.

MEDITATE ON PSALM 37:39–40

---

191 God Is Always Near

"When trees and power lines crashed around you, when the very roof gave way above you, when light turned to darkness and water turned to dust, did you call on Him?

"When you called on Him, was He somewhere up there, or was He as near as your very breath?

. . . "What some believers still can't believe is that it is God's passion to be as near to us as our very breath."

—*A New Song,* Jan Karon

In the times we feel alone with hard things pressing in, we can have peace that God is always near.

MEDITATE ON PSALM 34:18

192 I Just Need to Ask

Sarah stepped up, too, and held them both. "I don't know if I have the strength to let you go," she whispered.

"God will help you," Maggie said. "He's just waiting to be asked."

—*Seaside,* Terri Blackstock

God does not get frustrated or impatient when we ask for help. God is longing for us to ask and is more than willing to give us the guidance we seek.

MEDITATE ON JAMES 1:5

193 Talk It Over

"Then why do people pray at all? My papa asked Jesus to help him escape with me when I was just a little girl. But Jesus didn't help us."

"Praying ain't about asking for your own way. It's all about talking things over with God, just like you and me are talking things over. In the end, you have to be trusting the Lord to do what's best."

—*A Light to My Path,* Lynn Austin

Today is a great day to chat with God. I will share my heart with the Almighty and trust in all God has for me.

MEDITATE ON PSALM 37:5

---

194 Truth Is Easy

"I started a letter to him last night during a break from staring at the ceiling. I couldn't think."

Anna's chest rose and fell in an exaggerated sigh.

"I intend to tell him. It's hard to know what to say."

"Lies are complicated, Ivy. The truth is easy. It flows like maple sap on a warm spring day."

—*When the Morning Glory Blooms,* Cynthia Ruchti

Truth is always better than a lie. May God give me the strength to be a person of integrity so truth flows in all I say and do.

MEDITATE ON 1 CHRONICLES 29:17

---

195 Generosity of Listening

"I'll close with a very specific way to help you live the principle of outdoing. This is a key to opening hearts . . . Listen.

Listening is among the most generous ways to give. When a loved one talks to us—whether their words appear to be deep or shallow—listen. For in some way, they are baring their souls."

—*Come Rain or Come Shine,* Jan Karon

God shows me love by hearing me; I will show others love by hearing them.

MEDITATE ON PSALM 116:1–2

---

196 Get at the Roots

He'd lost a brother and had his reputation and calling taken from him. He was bitter about many things, but not about God. He still prayed constantly. Still went to church. Still reminded her that God loved her and was watching.

—*Truth Stained Lies,* Terri Blackstock

Bitterness is not something I want in my heart. I bring to God all that I am, asking the King to remove any root of bitterness from me.

MEDITATE ON HEBREWS 12:15

---

197 Praying from the Heart

*Luke swallowed. How often had he taken time to pray—***really** *pray—for guidance? He'd called out in anger and frustration, begged God to spare his life, but true, heartfelt, intentional prayer outside of a crisis? It'd been far too long.*

—*Dead Drift,* Dani Pettrey

God is ready for us in all things. We can pray in the hard times, but we can also pray from deep in our heart for guidance, encouragement, and hope.

MEDITATE ON PSALM 25:4–5

---

198 My Way to Heaven

"My dear Miss Keene, what would the world be without them?" He brushed the string from her cheek. "Are we not admonished to be doers and not merely hearers of His word? Yet not on a mountain of good deeds can we climb our way to heaven."

—*The Silent Governess,* Julie Klassen

God, You are my salvation. Help me rest firmly in Your grace, knowing it is by Your love that I can enter heaven.

MEDITATE ON EPHESIANS 2:8–9

---

199 Good Prevails

I do not believe that God has given us this trial to no purpose. I know that the day will come when we will clearly understand why this persecution with all its sufferings has been bestowed upon us—for everything that Our Lord does is for our good.

—*Silence*, Shūsaku Endō

Father, help me trust fully in You and Your ways. May I be confident that Your goodness will always prevail in my life.

MEDITATE ON 2 CORINTHIANS 9:18

---

200 Holy Spirit in Me

If God worked through her, then yes, she—one humble person—could maybe, she thought, quite possibly, hopefully . . . help many.

—*Undeniably Yours*, Becky Wade

I can do great things because the Holy Spirit lives in and works through me! I trust God to keep working through me, that I may do the will of the Father.

MEDITATE ON JOHN 14:12

---

201 Forgiven and Free

"I know it all sounds far-fetched. I've thought that too. That my mistakes . . . and there are an awful lot of them . . . couldn't possibly be erased clean. That Jesus couldn't possibly forgive them. But I think that's the whole point of why he came."

—*Truth Stained Lies,* Terri Blackstock

Nothing I do is too big, too awful, or too small for God's forgiveness. I am forgiven and free in Jesus!

MEDITATE ON LUKE 24:46–47

202 Trusting the Goodness of God

A year ago, she might have insisted it was all their fault. They seemed totally inept at dealing with the brokenhearted, kept trying to tell her life wasn't that bad.

Maybe it wasn't all them. Life could be enormously disappointing and still be good.

Did that thought live in her own head?

—*As Waters Gone By,* Cynthia Ruchti

I can trust God's goodness in all things, even more than my circumstances or feelings. God is good all the time.

MEDITATE ON 1 CHRONICLES 16:34

203 See Through His Eyes

*"And something you should remember for the future, Miss Laurent," Adelicia continued, her tone instructive. "Let no one define how you see yourself . . . save God alone. See yourself through His eyes and His strength, and you'll see who you **can** be despite being who you are."*

—*A Lasting Impression*, Tamera Alexander

What others think of us doesn't have to define us. Not even what we think of ourselves should define us. Today, we can walk freely in how God sees us!

MEDITATE ON ROMANS 8:16–17

---

204 Live Full

She frowned at him but nodded. "Yeah. When life seems to go south, we feel like God doesn't love us. But I keep going back to something my dad said to Owen. Maybe we have to start redefining how we understand God's love. And start hoping. My dad says that hope is one part confidence in God's love for us and one part our delight in Jesus."

—*It Had to Be You*, Susan May Warren

I will have confidence in God's love for me, freeing me to live full of hope in Jesus!

MEDITATE ON PROVERBS 14:26

---

205 Giving Up the Fight

"I'm sorry," Anna repeated. "You know, Chet. Some folks say God never gives us more than we can handle. I don't believe that's true. He doesn't give us more than He can handle. The battle belongs to the Lord. Let Him fight it for you."

—*Love Without End,* Robin Lee Hatcher

I choose to stop fighting battles on my own. I choose to let go of all that I hold on to and trust God to fight on my behalf.

MEDITATE ON 2 CHRONICLES 20:15

---

206 Taking Direction

Aurora's intensity challenged Susanna's comfort and notion of God's role in her life. "How do I hang on to my goals and plans without being so . . . "

"Uptight? You let him figure the outcome. We make our plans, but God directs our steps."

—*Once Upon a Prince,* Rachel Hauck

Today is a great day to trust God with the outcome of all my plans!

MEDITATE ON PROVERBS 16:9

---

207 Overcome Temptation

"It appeared at first drink. I was becoming the very thing I feared—my father's son. I wanted to be as far away from that Threshold as possible. I swore I'd never take another sip, no matter how crazy it made me. No matter how much it called to me. Resisting became easier with time."

—*Unblemished,* Sara Ella

No matter what temptations I face, I will bring them to God. The Lord promises to help me walk in the Spirit, victorious and holy.

MEDITATE ON GALATIANS 5:16–17

---

208 Find God

"Yahweh." Her voice trembled with passion. "Yahweh called to me . . . "

She smiled, her eyes traveling upward for a brief moment, as if she was remembering something from long ago. "Some- one once told me that Yahweh would make himself known to me, if I searched. And he did. Perhaps he will make himself known to **you***."*

—*Wings of the Wind,* Connilyn Cossette

I search for the Lord with all my heart and soul, full of faith I will find the God my heart longs for.

MEDITATE ON DEUTERONOMY 4:29

---

209 Healing in Love

"I know your stepmother did some bad things to you. She said things to you that weren't true." He spoke quietly, but unwaveringly. "My mother once told my sister, 'You must let God's love heal you.'"

Sophie touched his cheek, and he reached up and cradled her face in his hands. "You must let God's love and the blood of Jesus heal you of all those things the duchess said and did to you."

—*The Fairest Beauty*, Melanie Dickerson

The Lord comes in perfect love, healing the broken places in me so my soul may have deep, abiding peace.

MEDITATE ON JEREMIAH 33:6

---

210 Precious Friendships

She and Martine had not divulged the details of their pasts, for sharing the present had been enough. Their friendship had been woven from slender threads, with blank spaces where secrets were kept. It was precious, nonetheless. A piece of lace, gently worked. The empty places were as meaningful as the strands that embraced them.

—*A Refuge Assured*, Jocelyn Green

I am grateful for the precious friendships the Lord brings me. I will treasure each person God places in my life.

MEDITATE ON PHILIPPIANS 1:3–5

---

211 Living Each Day

Fanny smiled as she remembered times when as soon as Christmas had passed, she would tell her grandparents how she wished that it could instantly be summer.

"Do not wish your life away," Grandfather would tell her. "None of us know the number of days we are allotted. It would be foolish to discard any of them."

—*An Unexpected Love,* Tracie Peterson

Our days are a beautiful gift from God, but none of us knows how long we have here on this Earth. May I have the wisdom to live each day fully for God.

MEDITATE ON PSALM 144:4

212 More Than Prayer

"So what do I do?" Jake asked. "How do I convince her to trust in what we have?"

"You don't."

Jake loved his dad, but the cryptic answer made him grit his teeth. "But you did something, because here we are."

"By the grace of God, yes." Frank tossed the toothpick in the trash. "But it wasn't my doing. All I could do was pray."

"I remember that time, Dad. You did a lot more than pray. You and Mom went to counseling, and you stayed in church, even though you didn't like it sometimes."

—*The Two of Us,* Victoria Bylin

When I face something difficult, I have three things that will always help: prayer, church, and wise counsel.

MEDITATE ON ISAIAH 28:16

213 Listen Carefully

*Zack drew a deep breath and exhaled slowly. "Should
I come home?"*

*"Well . . . " His grandpa was quiet. "The situation with AJ isn't
an emergency." He hesitated. "Whatever God tells you . . . just
do that, son."*

*Tension tightened its grip on Zack's soul. "I'm trying. He keeps
moving me on to the next round."*

"Sometimes God's voice is hard to hear over the world."

—*Fifteen Minutes*, Karen Kingsbury

Hearing God's voice is more important than hearing any of
the other voices around me. I can ask God to help me hear
the one true Voice over all the others.

MEDITATE ON ISAIAH 28:23

214 A Solid Foundation

*She'd learned early to hold on tightly, to control her surround-
ings, her feelings. But control didn't buy safety . . . She didn't
need control. She needed to let go and trust God, and it was
hard. But He was her new foundation. She pictured it beneath
her, solid and unwavering. It would be okay.*

—*Driftwood Lane*, Denise Hunter

I don't need to control everything in my life. I can trust in God,
the unwavering foundation beneath me all of my days!

MEDITATE ON PROVERBS 11:14

215 Hearing God

If you want to know what God's plan is—then I would ask Him.
Couldn't hurt to search the Scriptures, too. And listen to what
He is telling you inside. Even when you don't think you're hear-
ing anything, keep listening. And know I'll be praying as well.
                    —*The Icecutter's Daughter,* Tracie Peterson

Prayer and God's Word are the best places to hear God and
learn God's best for my life. I will spend time meditating on the
promise that God hears me.

MEDITATE ON JEREMIAH 29:12
---

216 God Rejoices Over Me

"I'm almost afraid to be happy, especially in the midst of such
madness and uncertainty—as though it might be wrong. As
*though **I'm** wrong."*
"No, oh no, my Lea. Joy is the gift of God, and you are His child.
He loves you so. He rejoices over you with singing!"
                    —*Saving Amelie,* Cathy Gohlke

The Lord of all things rejoices over me! I am precious and
valued by God because of the perfect love and grace in
the Lord.

MEDITATE ON ISAIAH 62:5
---

217 Perfect Love and Forgiveness

But a few years ago, I went to a church service and the pastor happened to be preaching on the difference between divine forgiveness and human forgiveness. I knew I couldn't forgive others without God's help. He said that we fail in the work of grace and love when there is too much of us and not enough of God.

—*The Search,* Suzanne Woods Fisher

God's forgiveness is for me, fully and without exception. I lean on the perfect love and forgiveness of God to help me forgive others.

MEDITATE ON 1 TIMOTHY 1:15–16

---

218 Kindness and Help Go a Long Way

It seemed they had some of the supplies needed but definitely could use more financial and physical help. We arranged some of the former, while the boys filled in the latter . . . What they're doing is important. So often people think of sharing God's love by preaching or reading the Bible to someone. More often, we can show people Jesus by demonstrating kindness and love in practical ways.

—*A Matter of Heart,* Tracie Peterson

Jesus calls me to be kind and help others. Today I will show one person the love of Jesus by helping them in a practical way.

MEDITATE ON 1 JOHN 3:18

---

219 Taking the Risk

Buying that building was risky with income being so sporadic. But he'd learned long ago that a life without risks pretty much wasn't worth living. Life rewarded courage, even when that first step was taken neck-deep in fear.

—*Within My Heart,* Tamera Alexander

Even when things don't make sense, I can ask the Lord, my Great Provider, and trust the Lord will lead me in wisdom.

MEDITATE ON JOHN 21:6–11

---

220 The Hard Path Brings Life

"We will be surrounded by pain and suffering without the satisfaction of seeing them healed. You'll not be able to escape it on this ship. This is what you want?"

It would be difficult, Charlotte knew, but that was not reason enough to avoid it. "I want to help." Her tone was steeled with resolve.

—*Wedded to War,* Jocelyn Green

I will do whatever God calls me to do, even if it means choosing a hard path. Walking with the Lord brings life for me, no matter what I face.

MEDITATE ON MATTHEW 7:13–14

---

221 All Things Well

*"Always you focus on the dark side of things, my lady. You must
focus on the light, for there is much joy to be had in this world.
Open your eyes, and you will see it. And in time, all will be
well—for all of us."*

"You sound as if you truly believe that it will."

"Why shouldn't I?"

—From Darkness Won, Jill Williamson

My eyes are open to see the joy of God in my life! I trust the
Lord will make all things well.

MEDITATE ON ESTHER 8:15–17

222 When I Need to Wait

*It seems to me there are times when you have to act and times
when you have to wait, but the hardest times are those when
you want to do one but you have to do the other and you're not
sure which is best.*

—Almost Heaven, Chris Fabry

Waiting can feel so hard, but I trust the Lord to guide me in all
I do. Lord, help me wait patiently on Your timing in all things.

MEDITATE ON ACTS 1:4–8

223 Grateful for the Gift of Today

"Life is a gift, however long it lasts. It's God's to give and take away as He sees fit. We go through life thinking we're entitled to our ninety, but we're not entitled to anything. All we can do is trust that He knows what He's doing. That He has a plan for all of us, and that no pain He allows in our life will go unused. I suppose realizing that has given me a good measure of peace."
—*Barefoot Summer,* Denise Hunter

I'm so grateful for the gift of today. Lord, help me use it well for Your glory!

MEDITATE ON 2 CORINTHIANS 9:15

---

224 Be Ready

"How can one tell the difference between cold feet and trusting your gut, Father? How did you know your instincts about Willoughby were correct?"

"That's called faith. Trusting God." His voice waffled. "We must be ready to hear from Him and respond, at any moment, no matter what the consequence."
—*The Wedding Dress,* Rachel Hauck

Even when it feels hard, I choose to listen to the Lord, seeking the will of God in all I do.

MEDITATE ON MATTHEW 7:21

---

225 Relieved of My Past

"How can you say that? After all I've done?"

"Done. As in the past."

"Don't you know—'The past isn't forgotten. In fact, it isn't even past.'" Faulkner had it right.

"Bailey . . . " He said her name with so much love, her heart nearly broke. "You're a new creation. Your sins are forgiven. Why carry a burden Christ died to relieve you of?"

—*Submerged,* Dani Pettrey

I don't need to carry my past around with me like a weight. I can trust that Christ has relieved me of everything in my past.

MEDITATE ON EPHESIANS 4:22–24

226 Endless Love

"If only they knew how I still carry that burden of responsibility. I loved my brother. I loved my wife and son. For my parents to suggest or think otherwise broke me in a way I wasn't sure I could recover from."

. . . "I'm no preacher, but I do know that God doesn't strip away His love when we make mistakes."

—*A Matter of Heart,* Tracie Peterson

God, forgive me for holding on to my sin instead of giving my mistakes to you. I am grateful that You show me grace freely and without limits.

MEDITATE ON PSALM 103:12

227 My Life Is a Masterpiece

"Only Jesus can heal the wounds, only Jesus can fill up those dark places with light, with understanding. Only He can quench our thirst for hope."

Spencer's words drifted back to Rosie. **God has a plan, and it's so big and so good, He can take out all the mistakes and our hurts and weave them together to bring our life to full fruition. But I have to trust Him.**

—*Duchess*, Susan May Warren

My hope is in God, Who is using the difficult parts of my story to make my life a beautiful masterpiece!

MEDITATE ON PSALM 39:7

---

228 No More

"She'll think about it even if she walks away."

"I hope so. She believes it's an old woman's crutch. I told her it's better to go into heaven limping than not at all."

"There won't be any limping in that place." I smiled as my eyes watered again.

—*Higher Hope*, Robert Whitlow

The promises of heaven are for me. I will have no more pain or crying or death in heaven because God will wipe every tear from my eyes.

MEDITATE ON REVELATION 24:4

---

229 The Lord of My Life

I had to step aside and ask Someone else to do the fighting for me. And every time I thought of my particular battle—usually many times a day—I had to step consciously out of the way again and give gratitude to Him for the battle He was waging on my behalf right then. Sometimes it took days, sometimes longer, for evil was rarely flimsy but the outcome was sure; sure because He was and is the Lord of life.

—*Christy,* Catherine Marshall

I can rest and celebrate in the truth that God will fight my battles for me because God is the Lord of my life!

MEDITATE ON 2 CHRONICLES 20:17

230 Made New

All you need to do is ask, Jennia Beth Gibbs. No sense making a thief of yourself, now is there? You keep it . . . and remember that no matter how many wrong choices we've made in the past, we can always decide to make the right ones today. The past need not determine one moment of the future.

—*The Story Keeper,* Lisa Wingate

When we believe in Christ, we are a new creation. Remind yourself that you are a new creation in Jesus!

MEDITATE ON 2 CORINTHIANS 5:17

231 Hurt and Healing

Mack has been married to Nan for more than thirty-three mostly happy years . . . she seems to love him now more than ever, even though I get the sense that he hurt her something fierce in the early years. I suppose that since most of our hurts come through relationships, so will our healing, and I know that grace rarely makes sense for those looking in from the outside.

—*The Shack*, William Paul Young

Joseph and his brothers offer a beautiful story of healing relationships. Ask God to bring healing to a wounded relationship in your life.

MEDITATE ON GENESIS 37:12–36 AND 45:1–15

232 Talking from the Heart

"I'd said 'Now I lay me down to sleep' and 'Our Father who art in Heaven' and 'Give us this day our daily bread' a thousand times. But I'd never once prayed a prayer of my own until then. I believe that's when God first started speaking to my heart—the very day I started speaking to His!"

—*A Light in the Window*, Jan Karon

God longs to hear my voice. I will talk to the Lord from my heart today knowing the Lord cares.

MEDITATE ON PROVERBS 2:1–5

233 Take Time to Rest with God

You know how sometimes you walk outside, like out of a cold room, and the sun is coming up and it feels warm on your face? And all you want to do is stand there and soak it up? Well, that's kind of how I feel. I want to stand here and soak in this a while.

—*Thunder and Rain*, Charles Martin

No matter how busy things feel, it is good for me to take time to rest in the presence of God. My rest with the Lord is never a waste of time.

MEDITATE ON MARK 6:31–32

234 Saying Good-Bye

"We're not made to say good-bye. God didn't make us that way. We're eternal beings meant to live with him and those we love forever. So when we have to part with a loved one for a while because of death, it hurts."

—*Don't Look Back*, Lynette Eason

God longs for us to bring our grief and pain to Him, that we may know more of the Lord's great love. May I trust God with all that I am.

MEDITATE ON REVELATION 21:4

235 I Am Never Hidden

Ultimately, who we are can't be hidden. But here's the deal: when we face the worst that's in us, somehow we become better than we are—better than we ever thought we could be.
>   —*Healing Sands,* Nancy Rue and Stephen Arterburn

We are never hidden from God. Knowing I am known fully in God's grace brings me freedom.

MEDITATE ON HEBREWS 4:13,16

236 My Greatest Strength

I look at him. "Apparently you know the story," I mutter. "I don't have to tell you about it."
"Our weaknesses are poised to become our greatest strengths. If we are patient and if we believe, the switch will often happen when we most need it to."
>   —*The Day the Angels Fell,* Shawn Smucker

God works in my weakness! I walk in faith, trusting God will reveal strength at the right time for me.

MEDITATE ON PSALM 73:26

237 Changed for Good

"Everything's changed. Everything. Because I've changed. I'm not the man I was. I'm the man I see has already come alive in you. I'm discovering my true self and no longer living out of the lies about who I thought I was. The one who gets his validation from what he does is dying. The one who gets his validation from who he is, from who God sees he is—that's the man who is alive now."

—*The Five Times I Met Myself,* James L. Rubart

I am validated and alive in God, the One who sent the Holy Spirit to dwell in me.

MEDITATE ON 1 CORINTHIANS 3:16

---

238 Miracles in the Dark

She crossed her arms over her round abdomen.

Then she remembered something else Kiahna had written in her journal. Though her life hadn't turned out anything like she'd planned, she knew that in the darkest times God was always working. Always.

. . . **Times don't get much darker than this, God.** *Her gaze shifted to Max again. But what if Kiahna was right? What if somehow God was working out His best miracles even now, when life looked beyond hopeless?*

—*Oceans Apart,* Karen Kingsbury

Even in the darkest times, God is working out miraculous things. I can trust God even when everything around me feels hopeless.

MEDITATE ON MARK 5:35–42

---

239 | I Have Gifts

"Your identity doesn't come from your address."

"I know."

"Or your parents."

"I know that too." She did. But sometimes the knowledge failed to make the twelve-inch journey to her heart.

His thumbs moved over her cheek, sending shivers dancing down her spine. *"God made you special, Layla, inside and out. And He gifted you with an amazing talent."*

—*A December Bride,* Denise Hunter

Lord, show me the gifts You have given me, and help me use them confidently for You.

MEDITATE ON ROMANS 12:4–8

---

240 A Model of Forgiveness

I opened my mouth, my eyes on Rachel, and pushed out the words. A whisper. "I'm . . . so sorry."

She smiled, shook her head. "She forgave you . . . the moment you said it."

Forgiveness is a tough thing. Both in the offering . . . and the accepting.

—*The Mountain Between Us,* Charles Martin

We can use the model of Christ's forgiveness in our relationships. I will forgive freely and give myself permission to accept the forgiveness of God and others.

MEDITATE ON COLOSSIANS 3:13

241 What Makes Me Strong

"Are you reading your Bible?"

"Ah, well . . . I was."

"And then you quit."

"You got it."

"Then you can expect to be weak on one of your flanks, and that's precisely where the Enemy will come after you with a vengeance."

—*At Home in Mitford,* Jan Karon

The Bible is an essential part of my growth and strength. I will make time for God's Word, knowing it is important in my life.

MEDITATE ON 2 TIMOTHY 3:16–17

242 Undeserved Grace

"Let you down, did he?"

"You could say that."

Her grandma squeezed her arm, giving Daisy one of those pointed looks she was famous for. "You know honey . . . sometimes you just have to extend a little grace to people. Not because they deserve it—but because we don't deserve it either."

—*On Magnolia Lane,* Denise Hunter

I can show others grace because God has given me all the grace I will ever need!

MEDITATE ON LUKE 6:35–36
---

243 Dwelling with Me

The chill in the courtroom matched the chill in Seamus's soul. Hours of testimony and legal posturing had played out before him as he marked time by a wall clock. His every breath was a prayer. For peace. Protection. Truth.

Thy will be done.

—*The Mistress of Tall Acre,* Laura Frantz

All grace and truth and peace come from the Lord, Who dwells within me. I trust the will of God is being done in my life.

MEDITATE ON JOHN 1:14
---

244 Who God Is

"Hardships are the Lord's greatest blessings to the believer. Without them we would love the Lord only for what He does for us. Our troubles teach us to love Him for who He is."

Elizabeth bridled her response. Had she been serving the Lord for what He would do for her?

—*The Preacher's Bride,* Jody Hedlund

God is so much more than a fixer. I will serve the Lord fully, with my whole heart, not because of what the Lord does but because of who the Lord is.

MEDITATE ON DEUTERONOMY 11:13–15

245 Beautiful Details

Mom never cared much for poetry, said she had no use for it in what she faced every day, but the cadence of words speaks to me. Kind of stupid when you consider who I am and what I do. There is more to a soul than what others see.

—*Fire Dancer,* Colleen Coble

We were fashioned in amazing detail by the Creator of the universe. I am an amazing creation, full of wonder and beauty!

MEDITATE ON PSALM 139:13–16

246 In God's Strength

"You pray. And you allow the Lord to be your strength. Remember—the Lord doesn't give you strength, Hezekiah. He is your strength."

—Song of Redemption, Lynn Austin

I don't have to find strength on my own. I must only ask God to give me the strength I need for any situation. Thank You, God, for giving me Your strength!

MEDITATE ON PSALM 46:1

247 Finding My Comfort

Maybe it's God trying to comfort your heart. He does that, you know. The Holy Spirit is called the Comforter in the Bible. I reckon God wants us to find comfort and peace of mind, or He wouldn't have given us a Comforter.

—A Matter of Heart, Tracie Peterson

God longs for me to be comforted and find peace, and to share comfort with others. I choose to seek my comfort in the Holy Spirit today.

MEDITATE ON 2 CORINTHIANS 1:3-4

248 Being Part of a Family

"Everyone, even within a family, is different. We all have different needs, different issues we struggle with. Part of being a family is learning to face those differences, forgive, and accept so that you can move on to love."

—*Happily Ever After,* Susan May Warren

God gives us people to love and learn from. May I be one who recognizes the different needs in my family, forgiving often and loving them well.

MEDITATE ON EPHESIANS 3:14–15

249 When Loving Feels Hard

"Loving can be hard. Sometimes we don't feel loving, but it isn't all about feeling. Very often it's about will. Practice if you can." He thought he may have said too much, but he looked into their eyes, and knew he had not.

—*Home to Holly Springs,* Jan Karon

Even when it feels difficult to love, God calls us to love anyway. Ask God to help you love others well no matter the circumstances.

MEDITATE ON JOHN 13:34–35

250 God Will Hold My Pain

He stared away, past her, down the row. "I don't know why you went through what you did. But I do know this: I can suffer alone, or I can hold onto God in my pain. I can be meek and trust Him to make something good out of it."

—*Duchess*, Susan May Warren

We can bring our pain to God, asking the Lord to make something good out of it. Today I choose not to suffer alone. I welcome God.

MEDITATE ON ISAIAH 38:16–17

---

251 Tempered Through Fire

Delaney suspected those six Chinese Christians knew more about commitment to God, to steadfastness of faith, than dozens upon dozens of the believers he'd pastored through the years. Untested faith was rarely strong. Deep, abiding faith was tempered through fire.

—*Heart of Gold*, Robin Lee Hatcher

We don't need to fear when our faith is tested. We can rejoice that the testing will strengthen our faith in God.

MEDITATE ON ACTS 14:22

---

252 Without Understanding

"No, Meg, but people are more than just the way they look. Charles Wallace's difference isn't physical. It's in essence."

*Meg sighed heavily, took off her glasses and twirled them, put them back on again. "Well, I know Charles Wallace is different, and I know he's something **more**. I guess I'll just have to accept it without understanding it."*

—*A Wrinkle in Time,* Madeleine L'Engle

I can trust that God understands all I do not. I lean on the Lord to help me understand what I need.

MEDITATE ON ISAIAH 55:9

---

253 I Can Keep Going

What do you do when strength is called for and you have no strength? You evoke a power beyond your own and use stamina you did not know you had. You open your eyes in the morning grateful that you can see the sunlight of yet another day. You draw yourself to the edge of the bed and then put one foot in front of the other—and keep going.

—*Christy,* Catherine Marshall

I do not need to do anything in my own strength. I trust God to be the strength I need in all things as I keep moving forward in gratitude.

MEDITATE ON ISAIAH 40:29

---

254 Using the Scraps

"When things don't turn out the way we want," the dear woman said softly, "about the only thing we can do is know God is still there piecing together all the scraps of the events in our lives the way He has planned." Her chapped fingers lingered on an intricate pattern. "He sees the big picture even when we don't."

—*Unending Devotion,* Jody Hedlund

God has a plan for our lives. I can rise above broken dreams, disappointment, and heartbreak, knowing He is using every piece of my life to make something amazing!

MEDITATE ON ISAIAH 40:25–26

255 Finding True Peace

Isaiah slowly shook his head. "It's not about you. It's not about me. This life that we live, the reason we're here. It's only when we see our lives through eternal eyes that we find true peace or wealth that will last. Real security can only be found in that which can never be taken from you . . . in a relation-ship with God."

—*Rekindled,* Tamera Alexander

May we learn to rely on God for our true peace and security that will never fade. Seek the Lord anytime you feel uneasy and ask for perfect peace.

MEDITATE ON JOHN 16:33

256 Love Without Fear

"Love without fear . . . " Miss Foster murmured, considering the notion. "It doesn't sound very practical, I'm afraid. For the more one loves, the more one has to fear losing."

He looked at her, a grin tugging his mouth. "Impractical, maybe. Difficult, yes. But what a beautiful way to live."

—*The Secret of Pembrooke Park*, Julie Klassen

Loving deeply feels risky sometimes. But God's grace will help me let go of my fear to love fully.

MEDITATE ON 1 JOHN 4:18

---

257 The Strength I Need

"The one I'm really mad at is God. I try not to, but the truth is, when you boil it down, he let me get cancer."

"Humph," I said. "I always thought that God must trust you a lot to let you go through this."

Jeff flinched. "What do you mean?"

"Well, he knew you believed in him. He must have known how you would react. He trusted you to go through it."

Jeff frowned. "That's a thought. He's the one giving me strength. That's funny. I'm mad at the one giving me strength."

—*Grave Shadows*, Jerry B. Jenkins and Chris Fabry

Thank You for giving me strength in all things, Lord.

MEDITATE ON PHILIPPIANS 4:13

---

258 | Am a Reflection

He loved him now in a different way from before. Everything that had taken place until now had been necessary to bring him to this love. 'Even now I am the last priest in this land. But Our Lord was not silent. Even if he had been silent, my life until this day would have spoken of him.'

—*Silence,* Shūsaku Endō

My life is made to reflect the beauty, power, and glory of Jesus in all I do!

MEDITATE ON ROMANS 8:29

259 | Will Offer Welcome

Lillian wiped the tears that marred the carefully applied powder upon her cheeks. The pastor did not seem to notice. He took her hand in both of his and welcomed her. Welcomed her so warmly, in fact, that the tears fell even harder.

—*The Innocent Libertine,* T. Davis Bunn and Isabella Bunn

Thank you, Lord, for putting people in my life whom I can welcome and love, as You have done me. I will welcome others who come to me today.

MEDITATE ON 1 SAMUEL 25:6

260 Defining Success

"And now," he finally said, "nothing is more important to my dad than working hard and being successful."

"Is that what you believe too?"

"I guess."

"But you don't have to let his definition of success be yours."

         —Unending Devotion, Jody Hedlund

Jesus shows me how to live a successful life. May I meditate on these words and let Jesus's definition of success become my own.

MEDITATE ON MATTHEW 22:36–40

261 Loving God More Than Riches

"You will trust two women with your bank account?" Ivena asked with a raised brow.

"I would trust you with my life, Ivena."

"Yes, of course. But your money?"

"Money's nothing. You've said so a thousand times, dear."

         —When Heaven Weeps, Ted Dekker

I can trust God with all I have, even my money. May I live my life in a way that honors God and people as more important than money.

MEDITATE ON MATTHEW 6:24

262 Trusting God More Than My Feelings

Leena had a tenacity unlike any woman I'd ever met, and it was about to surface. While her emotions were very real and they gnawed at her with a raw sincerity, she was listening to something deeper. She was listening to her will, not letting what she felt dictate what she would do. Didn't let it dictate her life.

—*Water from My Heart*, Charles Martin

Solomon guides us to be led by God's wisdom instead of our thoughts and feelings. The Lord will show me how to live in Holy Wisdom today.

MEDITATE ON PROVERBS 28:26

---

263 God Gave Me Gifts

"Shall I give you advice as I did her?"

"Of course, Grandmother."

"Very well. Here is what I think. Don't let the world ever take away what makes you unique. And of even more importance, don't ever count your gift as a burden."

—*The Innocent Libertine*, T. Davis Bunn and Isabella Bunn

The Lord has chosen me and given me good gifts to use to serve the Lord and those around me. I praise God for who I am made to be!

MEDITATE ON 1 PETER 2:9

---

264 There Are No Lost Causes

"I admire your commitment to my education," he said as they meandered nowhere in particular.

"I only wish you were as committed to it as I am."

He chuckled. "I think you're attempting to reform a lost cause."

She shoved his arm playfully. "No one's a lost cause. You have just as much potential as anyone else."

—*Undaunted Hope,* Jody Hedlund

Thank You, Lord, that You never give up on me. There is nothing that could make You throw in the towel. Praise You. I am never a lost cause!

MEDITATE ON LUKE 15:4–7

265 To Be Forgiven

Thankful for the darkness and the noise of the wagon wheels over the prairie, Larson searched the night sky. Forgiveness was a strange gift. One that had to be shared in order to be kept. He might not understand everything the Bible said, but God's Word was clear on that point.

—*Rekindled,* Tamera Alexander

Teach me, Lord, to forgive others the way You forgive me.

MEDITATE ON MARK 11:25

266 Experience God Anew

The reverence in the room was tangible. The angels knew this moment for what it was. Holy and sacred. A heart was opening itself for the greatest gift of the universe, the presence of God.
—Miracle at the Higher Grounds Café, Max Lucado

Moses experienced the power of angels and the Spirit of God in Exodus. Imagine standing there with Moses and experiencing God in that way.

MEDITATE ON EXODUS 3:1–5

267 Ruler of the World

"I'm a believer. I've lived in the northern Rockies all my life, with my pa and the mountain men who were our friends. To my way of thinking, no one can live in the grandest cathedral on earth, the Rocky Mountains, and not know there's someone bigger than man in charge of the world."
—Petticoat Ranch, Mary Connealy

I declare the amazing power of God, the Almighty Creator for all that there was, is, and ever will be!

MEDITATE ON DANIEL 4:34–35

268 Put It in God's Hands

"What will tomorrow bring, dear Lord?" She raised her gaze to the heavens, the blackness stapled in place by the myriad of stars. "Take care of Solveig and Kaaren and the babes. Father, I leave them in your hands, for mine are far too small and weak. You are God, and I thank you."

—*A Land to Call Home*, Lauraine Snelling

I know my hands are too weak to hold those I love. I entrust them to God, asking the Great Comforter and Caretaker to keep them safe and show them great love.

MEDITATE ON NAHUM 1:7

269 Being a Peacekeeper

Even at eight years old, Mandy wanted to beg Ma not to fight. Ma was decent and strong. Pa was selfish and weak. The decent, strong person had to do decent, strong things like love unlovable people and keep peace even when it wasn't easy.

—*Doctor in Petticoats*, Mary Connealy

I have the opportunity to keep peace in hard situations and to love those who don't seem to deserve it. Lord, help me see those opportunities and walk in Your love.

MEDITATE ON ROMANS 14:19

270 I Was Made for This Moment

At long last Kenneth cleared his throat. "My friend, only you can know what God is speaking into your heart. But I can tell you this: God makes each one of us for the time into which we are born. He creates us for a purpose. Our job is to know Him well, discover what He created us to do, and then do it for all we're worth for the rest of our lives. Ask God to show you your purpose. He will answer."

—*Fit to Be Tied*, Robin Lee Hatcher

God created me to serve the Lord right at this moment!

MEDITATE ON ESTHER 4:13–14

271 Whatever Comes My Way

"When you can't trust others, and you can't trust yourself, you can always trust God. He'll carry you through whatever comes your way."

"Is it as simple as that?"

"Simple . . . yes." His lips tilted sideways. "Easy . . . no."

—*Falling Like Snowflakes*, Denise Hunter

I trust God, Who is always faithful to me, steadfast, and able to carry me through whatever comes my way.

MEDITATE ON ISAIAH 43:2

272 Lean In

He didn't wait to see if the duke followed. He walked as he'd learned to walk, with only a minimal limp, back straight, head held high in confidence rather than cockiness. He walked like a man who had learned to lean into God for whatever strength he needed.

—*Fit to Be Tied,* Robin Lee Hatcher

Whatever strength I need today, I lean into God, full of faith that the Lord will supply all I need.

MEDITATE ON PSALM 73:23–25

---

273 Time to Pray

"I've been praying for her."

He shot her a warm glance. "You're a good person, you know that?"

Serena let out a little laugh. "I'm not sure about that, but I believe God can do amazing things if his people will take the time to pray about them."

—*When a Heart Stops,* Lynette Eason

It's easy to think about praying or say you'll pray for someone, but sometimes we don't take time to actually talk to God. Take a few minutes right now to pray for someone.

MEDITATE ON ROMANS 12:12

---

274 A Simple God

*"Tell you what, just open your Bible," he once challenged
her. "Read and pray. You'll find treasure. Trust me. Your heart
will change."*

*Humble and simple, he made her see God was accessible. Even
eager to engage her.*

—*The Love Letter,* Rachel Hauck

God longs to engage with me! I don't need to say fancy words
or read certain books. I simply need to seek the Lord through
the Word.

MEDITATE ON PSALM 119:130

275 Finding My Treasure

*"I just want to finish this. Then I'm going to stop living my life
for my father and mother and start living it for myself."*

*"True treasure is inside your heart—it's a soul that is at peace
with God. So live this life for God, ah-tad. Not for your parents
or yourself. Streets of gold are for the next life."*

—*Deep Trouble,* Mary Connealy

I live my life for God while I look ahead to the good things God
has in store in heaven. That is where my true treasure lies!
May I live in full confidence of the good things to come.

MEDITATE ON REVELATION 21:21

276 Live in Peace

"Let's leave Gossamer Grove. May our obituaries someday say—preferably after we're dead of course—that we lived in peace, in love, and mostly in grace."

. . . Life was fragile, grace beautiful.

—*The Reckoning at Gossamer Pond,* Jaime Jo Wright

Lord, show me how to live in peace, love, and grace with those around me. I will do one thing that leads to peace today.

MEDITATE ON ROMANS 12:18

277 I Have a Destiny

*"You have a destiny. Do you know what it is? Are you willing to embrace it? Lay down your very life in its service . . . He knows exactly what he is doing in your life, and he has everything under control. You know that, but do you **believe** it? Will you go forward in the direction he has led you and rest in the knowledge that he'll see you through it?"*

—*The Shadow Within,* Karen Hancock

Lord, I want to trust Your plans for me. I want to walk forward in them, full of faith that You are guiding me every step of the way. Help me follow You in confidence.

MEDITATE ON HABAKKUK 2:3

278 | I Have Real Faith

"I used to think people who talked about God—Jesus—all that was crud . . . But that's not true. Not real faith. Real faith is knowing forgiveness comes, you change, and then you walk and struggle together . . . Life is hard and it takes guts, faith, and a massive amount of out-of-this-world grace."

—*The Reckoning at Gossamer Pond,* Jaime Jo Wright

I want to be a person of real faith, full of forgiveness and grace for all the things life has in store. God, give me Your grace and help others see You in all I do.

MEDITATE ON 1 PETER 5:10

---

279 The Secret Life

"Renny, there is a closet, actually more like a narrow room, that opens into the blue bedroom. I cleaned it out soon after I moved into the house, and I use it as a place to pray and meet with the Lord. The term **prayer closet** *comes from a verse in Matthew that says we are to go into our prayer closet and pray to our Father in secret. Jesus taught that the secret life we have with God is one of the true tests of the genuineness of our relationship with him."*

—*The List,* Robert Whitlow

Father, help me remember to set time and space aside to talk to You. I want to have a beautiful secret prayer life with You!

MEDITATE ON MATTHEW 6:6

---

280 Words for Me

The Lord's my shepherd . . .
She'd already memorized the short Psalm and was hungry for more. Indeed, each word seemed woven into her soul the way the weaver wove his wares, taking the barest threads of her faith and making something beautiful and enduring as fine cloth deep inside her . . . These were her words—holy words.

—*Love's Reckoning,* Laura Frantz

I will read and rest in God's Word today. The Word is for me, weaving together the most beautiful parts of who God is.

MEDITATE ON PSALM 23:1–6

---

281 An Unlikely Celebration

Here's the truth: No matter what happened on the stage tonight, no matter where you went when you drove out of here, no matter where you end up, no matter what happens, what you become, what you gain, what you lose, whether you succeed or fail, stand or fall, no matter what you dip your hands into . . . no gone is too far gone.

You can always come home.

And when you do, you'll find me standing right here, arms wide, eyes searching for your return.

I love you.

—*Long Way Gone*, Charles Martin

Think of a time you've been lost or off track in your life. Now, picture God, the Father, celebrating your return. Remind yourself: I trust that God is waiting for me every single time I come back.

MEDITATE ON LUKE 15:11–32

---

282 Walking Through a Struggle

" . . . The whole point of the work of Jesus, the whole reason for His sinless life, the reason for the miracles and raising Him from the dead was the glory of God . . .

"Wrap your heart around that the next time you go through a struggle," Clara said. "The goal of prayer is to change your own heart, to want what He wants, to the glory of God."

—*War Room*, Chris Fabry

We can bring glory to God in all things. God, change my heart as I come in prayer, that I may bring glory to You.

MEDITATE ON DEUTERONOMY 5:24

---

283 Believing Even When I Don't Understand

One of her greatest fears had been close to happening and she wasn't sure how to deal with it. Praying helped, but she had to admit, her faith was wobbling. She might say all the right things, and truthfully, she really did believe them, but . . . it was hard to understand what God was doing.

—*Without Warning,* Lynette Eason

As much as we want to understand God, sometimes we can't. That doesn't mean we don't trust the Lord; it just means we are human.

MEDITATE ON ECCLESIASTES 11:5

284 Beauty All Around

Shannon leaned forward and rested her head on his strong shoulder. "You're a man of faith, aren't you?"

"I've seen too much of the beauty of the Lord's creation to ever doubt the Almighty."

—*Now and Forever,* Mary Connealy

As we look around, we are surrounded by the beauty of the Lord's creation. Thank God for something beautiful around you today.

MEDITATE ON PSALM 95:4–5

285 The Value of Friendship

"You've known me such a short time."

"Not all friendships take a long time to grow and deepen. Some are formed in an instant." Her smile broadened now. "From the moment we met, I knew we were destined to be good friends. I'm not sure why. It's just the way I felt."

—*Belonging,* Robin Lee Hatcher

I am so grateful for the friendships in my life! May God bring me people who become truly good friends, that our friendship may bring honor to the Lord.

MEDITATE ON PROVERBS 18:24

286 Come into the Storm

*I'd wanted—no, expected—God to rescue me, to make the troubles stop and go away, to restore my life to what it used to be. But here in this room, on my knees, I realized that I needed God more than I needed rescuing. I need to draw closer to Him **in** the storm more than I needed to be taken **out** of the storm.*

—*The Perfect Life,* Robin Lee Hatcher

Lord, thank You for being with me in the middle of the storms I face today! In this prayer, I draw close to You.

MEDITATE ON JAMES 4:8

287 I'm Not Worthy

"But I'm not worthy." She hung her head, letting her hair curtain her face.

"Ah, there's the rub." He bent to see her eyes. *"You're making this about your worthiness instead of God's. None of us are worthy. Do you think I'm worthy to be a reverend? To pastor His flock?"*

—*A March Bride*, Rachel Hauck

What a relief that I don't need to rely on my own worthiness! I stand firmly on the worthiness of God today.

MEDITATE ON ROMANS 3:21–26

288 A Strong Relationship

"I think some people can start out having a passion for God, but if that passion isn't flamed, disciple, or encouraged, it can—" She stopped as though searching for a word.

"Fizzle out?"

"Yeah. Don't you think? I mean, having a relationship with God still takes work on our part. If you ignore it long enough, it will wither and die. I'm talking about on the human end, not God's."

—*When a Secret Kills*, Lynette Eason

Lord, help me abide in You, that my relationship with You stays strong and healthy!

MEDITATE ON JOHN 15:4–5

289 Standing for the Oppressed

"There's a fire in you, Julie. I can see you out there in the street, carrying a banner for all the underprivileged people of the world."

—*Julie,* Catherine Marshall

The Lord longs for us to be advocates, standing up for the oppressed. Today I will use my prayer, my voice, and my actions to declare love to the underprivileged.

MEDITATE ON ISAIAH 1:17

---

290 Tell the Truth

"Just keep telling yourself the truth. Your emotions will catch up eventually."

"The truth," Lucy whispered as she swallowed against the pain at the back of her throat. "I don't even know what that is anymore."

Eden squeezed her hand. "Be patient. Pray about it, and listen to God. He'll help you figure it out."

—*The Goodbye Bride,* Denise Hunter

We can bring all our feelings to the Lord. When we remember truth, we can pray in faith and listen to God, confident the Lord will help us.

MEDITATE ON JEREMIAH 33:3

---

291 The Majesty of God

"Don't try to comprehend with your mind. Your minds are very limited. Use your intuition. Think of the size of your galaxy. Now, think of your sun. It's a star, and it is a great deal smaller than the entire galaxy . . . think of yourselves, now, in comparison with the size of your sun. Think how much smaller you are."

—*A Wind in the Door,* Madeleine L'Engle

The Lord is bigger and more powerful than I can fathom. I praise God, the Majestic One!

MEDITATE ON PSALM 147:5

292 Without a Doubt

He stepped into the shower's warm rush, his head pounding. This was too much debate for so early in the day.

The water ran down his shoulders as he bowed his head and baptized himself with prayer. If he was going to figure out his life, he had a feeling he needed more time on his knees, lifting up holy hands without doubt.

—*The Memory House,* Rachel Hauck

Help me come to You, Lord, in full faith. May I be one who prays to You in all things and may You take away my doubt.

MEDITATE ON JOHN 20:24–29

293 | I Am Weak

*"'Face the truth, Ken,' he told me. 'You **are** weak. All of us are.
Come to terms with it.'*

*"But then he pointed out I didn't have to stay this way, that God
was certainly not weak. Dean has helped me understand that
if I have the Spirit of God within me, then His strength would
replace my weakness."*

—*Julie*, Catherine Marshall

I open myself for God's grace and love to replace all my
weakness with a perfect, holy strength.

MEDITATE ON 2 CORINTHIANS 12:9–10

---

294 Hand Them Over

*She was determined to be in control. To not let what William
did control her.*

Her frustration flared.

*But that was exactly the problem. She was trying to control
what she couldn't because she wasn't the one in control. God
was. Maybe it was time she handed her hurts and fears fully
over to Him.*

—*Sabotaged*, Dani Pettrey

The Lord wants us to let go of our fears, trusting the God of
the Universe to handle all things, all the time. I can trust God
with my hurts and fears.

MEDITATE ON JEREMIAH 32:27

---

295 Be Salty

"Lord, we need a generation of believers who are not ashamed of the gospel. We need an army of believers who hate to be lukewarm and will stand on Your Word above all else. Raise 'em up, Lord. Raise them up."

—*War Room,* Chris Fabry

We are called to be the salt of the earth. Lord, I will stay true to You and show Your love to the people around me each day.

MEDITATE ON MATTHEW 5:13

296 Rely on the Creator

On the days Walter came to her apartment, to write down the stories of her butterflies, he always prayed with her, that in their weaknesses—both his and hers—God would be strong. That she would rely on the Creator more than her own creation.

—*Shadows of Ladenbrooke Manor,* Melanie Dobson

My Creator, I keep my eyes on You. I can trust Your strength and presence in my life always. You are faithful.

MEDITATE ON 1 CHRONICLES 16:11

297 Be Present

Ben leaned against the dresser, his arms still crossed. "You want my two cents?"

"Two cents doesn't buy much these days."

"You shouldn't let something that happened in the past stop you from having something that could be great in the present."

—*The Art of Losing Yourself,* Katie Ganshert

I will meditate on the new things God is doing in my life instead of dwelling on the past. God promises good for me and I trust the Lord.

MEDITATE ON ISAIAH 65:17

---

298 Using the Struggles

The marriage rope swung and she and Tony were trying hard to keep both feet above it as it crossed between them. The finance rope also swung over them, and the spiritual rope—there were just so many ways to trip and get tangled . . . God used it all. He used the hard times to draw her closer. He used the struggle to bring them together.

—*War Room,* Chris Fabry

Thank You, God, for using all the struggles in my life to draw me closer to You!

MEDITATE ON ROMANS 8:18

---

299 Practical Gratitude

"My father always told us . . . that if we will let God, He can use even our disappointments, even our annoyances to bring us a blessing. There's a practical way to start the process too: by thanking Him for whatever happens, no matter how disagreeable it seems."

—*Christy*, Catherine Marshall

I will thank God for whatever happens to me today, trusting that the Almighty knows exactly what is best.

MEDITATE ON 1 TIMOTHY 4:4–5

---

300 Clear-Cut Faith

"It's been the delight of my life to find God far more common sense and practical than any human I know. The only time I ever find my dealings with God less than clear-cut is when I'm not being honest with Him. The fuzziness is always on my side, not His."

—*Christy*, Catherine Marshall

Lord, thank You for being so clear and faithful in my life. Help me trust You as El Roi, the God who sees.

MEDITATE ON HEBREWS 10:23

---

301 A Place of Worship

"Lord, wherever I go, may I make the court of law a place of praise."

It was a beautiful thought. To find a place of holiness in the midst of a secular courtroom was something I'd never considered, and I marveled at a new facet of God's greatness. I might not shout "Hallelujah" in a judge's face, but my soul, like Mary's, could magnify the Lord, and my spirit could rejoice in God, my Savior. And the truth was even greater than that. Wherever I set my foot, not just a courtroom, could be a place of worship.

—*Deeper Water*, Robert Whitlow

The Holy Spirit comes with me wherever I go. Everyplace I go can be a place of worship and praise!

MEDITATE ON JOSHUA 5:15

---

302 Knowing Who I Am

"I don't know, Pop. It sort of seems like I lost the right to speak on the subject. Who am I to stand up in front of a large audience and dole out marital advice when I was having problems of my own?"

. . . "You know what I think?" Pop said, scratching the whiskers on his chin again. "I think that the second we find ourselves asking 'Who am I?' is the second we become the perfect person for the job."

—*Life After*, Katie Ganshert

My identity is not in who I am or what I can do. My identity is rooted firmly in Jesus.

MEDITATE ON 1 CORINTHIANS 6:17

---

303 I Am Gifted

Her floor was covered with pictures and papers, but where others might see a mess, she saw a new world. There were flowers and trees and butterflies she'd brought to life with her hands. And her heart.

A lot of people thought she wasn't good at anything, but it wasn't true. She was good at making things.

—*Shadows of Ladenbrooke Manor*, Melanie Dobson

Thank You for the unique gifts You have given me! Help me embrace my gifts and use them for Your glory in all I do.

MEDITATE ON 1 CORINTHIANS 12:4–6

---

304 The Best Weapon

"Benaiah's son fought with a sword and spear, but my daughter will bring her own weapon to the palace."

"I'm sorry, Jehoshaphat," Ahishar said. "I must draw the line here. None of the king's wives are permitted to keep weapons in their private chambers . . . "

"As I was saying, King Solomon," Jehoshaphat interrupted, ignoring the steward, "my daughter brings with her the most powerful weapon on earth—love."

—*Love's Sacred Song*, Mesu Andrews

Love is always the perfect answer. God, show me how to live my life in the strength of Your love to fight against all that is not Your best.

MEDITATE ON COLOSSIANS 3:14

---

305 God Will Restore Hope

Now I feel it in the part of me that can't explain the events of this watershed year in any other way—the truth of infinite possibilities. No stretch of the imagination, no far-flung splinter of hope is too remote for God. If I've learned one thing, that is it.
—The Story Keeper, Lisa Wingate

Have hope today, even if things seem to be falling apart. Even Job, who had lost a great deal, held on to hope in God.

MEDITATE ON JOB 42:2

306 Comfort in Endurance

You weep with those who gently close the eyes of the dead, and somehow, from the salt of your tears, comes endurance for them and for you. You pour out that resurgence to minister to the living.
—Christy, Catherine Marshall

The Lord is my Great Comforter in all things. May I receive comfort from the Lord and offer the same to those around me who are hurting.

MEDITATE ON PSALM 119:28

307 Trust the Promises

"You can have it too. The same Holy Spirit, the same forgiveness, the same love."

Maureen pulled back, fighting the rising tide of darkness, the swell of futility. **You mean well, but you can't know; you don't understand.** *"Good night, Olivia." Five steps brought her to the door.*

"It isn't because of who I am, Maureen. It's because of who He is and what He's done—what He longs to do in you!"

—*Band of Sisters*, Cathy Gohlke

Lord, I receive your Holy Spirit. Even when I don't feel like I deserve all You offer, I trust Your promises of forgiveness and love.

MEDITATE ON ISAIAH 1:18

---

308 Believe in the Plan

"No, my girl. Never be grateful for tragedy, but always trust that God can use it in His good plan for you." She knew she sounded so wise, so sure of God. But how could she tell a girl who already doubted El Shaddai that even His prophetess now struggled to understand Him?

Taliah pulled her hand away. "If this is your God's plan, I don't like it."

"Our God always has a plan. We just don't always know it."

—*Miriam*, Mesu Andrews

Lord, I want nothing more than to trust in You. Sometimes it feels hard, but I still choose You. I choose to have faith in Your plan.

MEDITATE ON PSALM 40:4

---

309 A Grateful Child

"I started by spending time thanking God for his past love and faithfulness. Although completely sufficient in himself, the Lord, like any parent, appreciated the thanks of a grateful child."
—*Deeper Water*, Robert Whitlow

God delights in our gratitude. We can show our love as we thank the Lord in all things. Thank God for all the love the Lord has given you today.

MEDITATE ON PSALM 136:26

---

310 Enduring Obedience

"How can you be so accepting? How is it that you are not screaming with frustration?"

"I've been spending more time in prayer. I am learning that obedience to God means that you do not put your eyes on your longings, but instead, you simply place one foot ahead of the other into the space that the Lord opens. Tired, wounded, overwhelmed. It does not matter. You merely keep moving where God directs and stop focusing on what you wish you had. It's teaching me patience."
—*Land of Silence*, Tessa Afshar

Father, give me the endurance to obey Your commands in all things so I won't grow weary of doing what is right. I will be patient and focus on You.

MEDITATE ON REVELATION 14:12

---

311 Knowing When to Fight

Ingrid straightened her shirt, which had gone askew in the battle, and took my offering. "Not all things are worth saving, you know. But some are worth every ounce of fight you can throw at them." With all the dignity in the world she took a few small bites of her dessert. "You just have to know the difference."
> —*The Art of Losing Yourself,* Katie Ganshert

I can ask God for wisdom to know and understand which things I should fight for. God is faithful and will answer my prayers.

MEDITATE ON COLOSSIANS 2:2–3

---

312 I Need Rescue

"Jeremiah, I've tried," she protested. "All I do is stumble about, making everything worse. I see no way through this—"

He held up a hand, stopping her. "I've been where you are. I've felt what you're feeling. But you must surrender your will and your wisdom to the Almighty, give it over to Him once and for all and stop blindly groping about for what to do next. Why not try doing **nothing***?"*

She looked at him uncomprehendingly.

"I don't think you grasp what it means to wait on the Lord,"
he said. "To let Him come to your rescue. To completely, utterly trust."
> —*Many Sparrows,* Lori Benton

I can stop trying to rescue myself and allow the Lord to come to my rescue!

MEDITATE ON COLOSSIANS 1:13–14

---

313 Trusting God

"Just trust me."

"You say it like it's so easy."

Evan spun her around him. "Of course it's not."

"Then how am I supposed to 'just trust' you?"

"Funny thing about trust." He let go of one of her hands and made her move in a way she didn't think possible. Her eyes widened. "Sometimes you have to give it before you can experience it."

—*Wildflowers from Winter,* Katie Ganshert

I trust in God because the Lord will never let me down!

MEDITATE ON PROVERBS 29:25

314 Grace for a Fresh Start

"I think that's what a fresh start is all about. Not ignoring the past, but seeing it through the eyes of God, through the eyes of grace. Knowing where we've been and where we're going. A fresh start isn't about forgetting; it's about perspective."

—*Licensed for Trouble,* Susan May Warren

God can help me see my past through His eyes of grace, giving me hope for a fresh start in all that is to come.

MEDITATE ON REVELATION 21:5

315 Equipped for the Path

"The path Creator has laid for us to walk," Clear Day went on, as though he'd read her thoughts, "has not been an easy path. Not always straight. And it will not be easy in the coming days. But when Creator said He would make rough ways smooth, I believe He was not talking about moving us to an easy path. He meant He was going to make our stride long enough, our legs strong enough, to carry us through. And when we reach our limits, He puts us on His back and He carries us and shields our eyes and hearts from that which would destroy our souls."

—*A Flight of Arrows*, Lori Benton

The Creator gives me all I need to walk the path laid out before me. When I don't feel I can continue, the Lord will carry me.

MEDITATE ON ISAIAH 40:11 AND 42:16

---

316 Not Left to Chance

" . . . What are the chances of such a configuration of far-fetched circumstances?"

"None! There is no chance at work here, my dear. This is a door that the Lord holds open for you. Walk through it. He who has called shall also equip. Everything you lack shall be provided."

—*Harvest of Rubies*, Tessa Afshar

My life is not left to chance. The God of the Universe is in complete control and will equip me for all that is put before me!

MEDITATE ON HEBREWS 13:21

---

317 Listen to the Spirit

"Wow, you startled me."

"Sorry, I woke up and you weren't in bed. Are you okay?"

"Fine, just trying to figure out what I'm preaching on this Sunday." Mark stretched his neck to the right and then the left. *"And I'm a little tense."*

"What's on your heart?"

"What?"

"On your heart, what are you hearing from God?"

—*The Chair*, James L. Rubart

The Holy Spirit speaks to my heart and I listen intently for all that the Spirit of God says to me.

MEDITATE ON PSALM 85:8

---

318 A Symbol of Hope

"I don't think you were messed up; I think the situation you were born into was. But you know something? God has a way of taking messed-up situations and flipping them on their heads."

"Oh yeah? Give me one example."

"Turning an executioner's cross into a symbol of hope."

—*A Broken Kind of Beautiful*, Katie Ganshert

Your cross brings my complete freedom, Lord! Thank You, Father, for my salvation in You.

MEDITATE ON GALATIANS 3:13–14

---

319 God's Understanding Is Greater

"You've never been in control of this situation. Nor have I," he added, seeing accusation fill her gaze. *"The Almighty is in control."*

"And a fine job He's done of things thus far!"

"Clare . . . Don't go judging the Almighty by your own under-standing. We're rarely given eyes to see the whole of what He's doing in our lives or through us. That's why we're called to walk by faith, not by sight."

—*Many Sparrows*, Lori Benton

I trust in the control of the Almighty and surrender all that I am and all that I understand, in full faith.

MEDITATE ON JOHN 13:6–9

---

320 Seasons of My Life

"I love all the seasons, I suppose. Spring because it is a time of new life, when the bulbs and berries that have been waiting for a bit of warmth suddenly start bursting with vitality. In the summer the transformation slows, but we work to nurture all the new life around us. And then autumn is a time of reaping the rewards for hard work, for digging in the soil to find the dense, nourishing root vegetables that will sustain us through the winter. It seems like everything sleeps in winter, but it's really a time of renewal and reflection."

—*Until the Dawn*, Elizabeth Camden

I trust that everything has a season. God will order every season of my life in wisdom and love.

MEDITATE ON ECCLESIASTES 3:1–8

321 Trust and Pray

"I will trust, I will pray, and no more," she whispered into the blanket's muffling folds. *"Even if it means I must grieve Jacob and pass through life and death to see him again. I believe You have him, have us all, in Your hands. You're doing what You will, and it will be for the best."*

But help my poor battered heart. Give me strength to do this.

—*Many Sparrows*, Lori Benton

I trust God with the most tender places of my heart. The Lord gives me strength to trust, pray, and be at peace with the will of God.

MEDITATE ON 1 PETER 5:7

322 Threads of Grace

Naomi enfolded Ruth in a warm embrace, before drawing back and patting her cheek. "If God spared us from the piercing shaft of every sorrow," she said, "we could never fulfill His best plans for our lives. Sometimes the sweetest things in life rise up out of the worst things in life."

—*In the Field of Grace*, Tessa Afshar

I will look for threads of grace in my life, the evidence of God's redemption in the hard places that reveal something wonderful.

MEDITATE ON RUTH 4:14–15

---

323 Show God's Love

She had learned a long time ago not to argue theology. She hadn't come to faith because someone gave her all the answers. She came to faith because she met and talked with someone who made her feel enveloped by God's love.

—*The Masterpiece*, Francine Rivers

The King is so kind to send people who model love for me. I will thank God for someone who models love, and I will be that person to others.

MEDITATE ON ROMANS 12:9–10

---

324 Persevere in All Things

"There will always be storms, Shira. There will be loss in your life, sometimes devastating loss. But if you let the wind and the rain overcome you, then you will never fulfill the purpose for which you were born, the reason Yahweh gave you breath and brought you to this time, to this place. There will be times when there is nothing you can do but survive, to place one foot after the other into the driving rain."

Her thin lips flattened. "You can tuck your head under your wing for a while, Shira, and wait out this storm. But you will fly again."

—*Shadow of the Storm,* Connilyn Cossette

We can hold on to hope, even in the hardest times. God has promised me a crown of life in the Lord.

MEDITATE ON JAMES 1:12

---

325 The Perfect Love of God

I'd do anything for them. How did I miss it? This entire time I've been closing myself off from love, but it's been the solution all along. I've built walls at every turn. No more. As with Queen Ember, drawn to her king from another Reflection, it isn't song alone that ignites my Calling, but love. True, unblemished love.

—*Unblemished,* Sara Ella

God is perfect love. I come to the Lord to know love, be loved, and love others.

MEDITATE ON 1 JOHN 4:7–8

---

326 Hope in the Lord

*"And what of you?" She turned her face to me, brows drawn and
a frown across her lips, as if her unseeing eyes could peer at my
heart and read the resignation scrawled across its surface.*

*I sighed. "As you said. I've endured this hardship for all these
years. I will continue."*

*"If there is one thing I've learned in my life, it's that one can
either endure hardship or thrive within it."*

—*A Light on the Hill*, Connilyn Cossette

I stand on the promise that I have life in Christ. Nothing I face
can change the hope I have in the Lord!

MEDITATE ON LUKE 21:19

327 Free from Bitterness

*We wiggled quietly in the dark, and I was glad that it felt natural
and free to be laughing with my mother. Somehow it seemed
as though the journey through the sea had washed my heart of
bitterness toward her and filled the empty places with a sooth-
ing tranquility. Strange that although we still wandered in a
desert of uncertainty, I had never felt more at home.*

—*Counted with the Stars*, Connilyn Cossette

I let go of any bitterness in my life, forgiving people freely and
showing kindness just as Christ has shown to me.

MEDITATE ON EPHESIANS 4:31–32

328 Peace for Us All

"Life is full of heartache and hardship," she says. "Very rarely will life make sense, and it will almost never seem fair. But if you remember that pain and heartache aren't unique to only you, that you're not the only one mired in circumstances that seem too great to bear, you'll do much better in life."

—*Like a River from Its Course*, Kelli Stuart

When things don't make sense and feel painful, I trust that God brings peace deep into my soul.

MEDITATE ON JOHN 14:27

329 Bring It All to God

"Thank you. And now, please go home to rest. You have done all you can for me, and I thank you."
Slowly, Francoise stood and pinned her lace cap to her curls. "Talk to the Lord, Julianne. Even if you're mad as hornets. If you keep it all bottled up, you'll only end up with a belly full of bee stings."

—*The Mark of the King*, Jocelyn Green

I bring all my thoughts and feelings to the Lord, the One who will comfort my soul.

MEDITATE ON 2 CORINTHIANS 1:5–6

330 He Cares for Me

"Do troubles bring us closer to God? The answer is yes, they do, but we must choose it. Otherwise, our troubles do just the opposite. They push us away from God. 'Cast all your anxiety on Him because He cares for you.'"

His voice had gradually softened with each word he spoke, until it was deep and rich, like the sound of thunder in the distance.

—The Merchant's Daughter, Melanie Dickerson

God cares for me and offers to take all my worries and fears. I have peace knowing the Lord is always here.

MEDITATE ON 2 THESSALONIANS 3:16

331 Healing in Tears

I started weeping, full of so many emotions. Regret. Sadness. Relief. Abra reached over and held on to my hand. It hurt, but I did not pull away . . . There is healing, after all, in sadness, and sometimes only tears will bring it. Abra's grip reminded me that I was human. I was here. I felt real again. I felt alive.

—The Day the Angels Fell, Shawn Smucker

I do not need to be afraid of hard feelings. I bring them to God, trusting the healing power of the Lord in my tears.

MEDITATE ON PSALM 30:5

332 My Peace in Darkness

I think of our life before the bombs, the river of our days flowing so calmly in a direction that I thought would last forever. In a flash, that river was turned, unexpected and quick, dragging us along this unforeseen path. Like a river from its course, life has swirled away from all I expected or planned. Sluggish and slow, this river carves a new path. There are calmer waters that wait.

—*Like a River from Its Course*, Kelli Stuart

No matter the course of our lives, God promises to be with us. The Lord shines in my darkness and brings me peace.

MEDITATE ON LUKE 1:78–79

---

333 The Movement of Time

Was Fern right? Was she hiding behind her fears? She looked over at the bakery counter. Was spending most of her time in the kitchen just another way to hide?

Fern reached out and covered Sadie's hand with hers, a rare display of affection. "Sadie girl, don't waste these years. Time is like the Mississippi River. It only flows in one direction. You can never go back."

—*The Keeper*, Suzanne Woods Fisher

Father, help me make the most of my time, being alert to Your will and ways for my life.

MEDITATE ON EPHESIANS 5:15–17

---

334 Walk in Wisdom

Over the next solid hour, Olivia spilled more beans than Adella could have shoveled back into a ten-gallon can. Some of what she said was incoherent and some of it fragmented, but the part about her son spoke a language between two mothers where words were unnecessary . . .

Sometimes all you could do for the suffering was to make sure they knew someone was suffering right there with them. Someone who had also felt stricken, and smitten, and afflicted.

—*The Undoing of Saint Silvanus*, Beth Moore

I listen to God and to others, walking through suffering with them in wisdom and love, just as the Lord walks with me.

MEDITATE ON PROVERBS 1:5

335 An Unchanging God

"Life isn't just guesswork."

"And faith isn't just feeling. We have to know He's still there, unchanged, even when we can't feel Him. When the grief's too loud to let us hear His voice."

—*The Number of Love*, Roseanna M. White

The Lord is always with me, no matter what my feelings tell me. I trust in the unchanging God of my heart.

MEDITATE ON HEBREWS 13:6

336 Ease My Pain

With her hand pressed to her heart, Julianne trapped a groan in her chest. "Does the pain ease?" she whispered.

Francoise sighed. "The pain changes, and you will change with it. The sharp edges wear away in time, but the loss remains. You'll learn how to live with it. There's not a day that goes by that I don't think of my little girl, and I warrant you won't forget your son. Never, as long as you live. And when we get to heaven, our little ones will know their mamas. I believe God Almighty and the Blessed Virgin, who also knows what it is to lose a child, will see to that."

—*The Mark of the King,* Jocelyn Green

Lord, heal the broken places in my heart and ease my pain, that I may have hope in You.

MEDITATE ON PSALM 147:3

---

337 God Wants All of Me

"Either you trust Him or you don't."

Achan shifted on his chair. "Maybe I don't then."

"I agree. You don't trust Him fully or you'd know you did. Arman wants your trust, Highness. When He asks something of you, He's seeking your heart. Your attitude, your disposition, your fears, your strengths, your obedience, your allegiance. All of you."

—From Darkness Won, Jill Williamson

God desires all that I am, all that I think, all that I feel. I give myself fully to the Lord, resting in the promise of eternal life with the King!

MEDITATE ON ROMANS 6:22

---

338 No One Is Too Small

"Do not pretend this was a simple birth. Thank you. If you hadn't been here—"

"But she was." Francoise bent and kissed Denise's temple and then the baby's velvety head. "And so was God, who faithfully guided her . . . There is no person so small that the Lord cannot see her, no voice so quiet that He cannot hear it."

—The Mark of the King, Jocelyn Green

God always sees me and hears all I say. The Lord cares about every part of who I am.

MEDITATE ON MATTHEW 10:29–31

---

339 The Work of My Hands

"God is the Creator, is He not?" *she had said with a smile.* **"So when we create, even if it is a mere length of lace and not the stars in the heavens, we honor Him. We bear His likeness when we work."** *That truth had lingered in Vienne ever since. When the government turned cathedrals into houses of reason, and when the church bells ceased to ring, Vienne had still quietly honored the Lord with the work of her hands.*

—*A Refuge Assured,* Jocelyn Green

I serve the Lord with the work of my hands. Any creative gifts I have are for the Glory of God.

MEDITATE ON EXODUS 35:31–35

340 Prayer Heals My Soul

"Prayer is not a magician's trick. The changes it brings cannot always be seen at first glance. But just as slippery elm soothes inflammation, prayer is a balm for a raw and ragged soul. And isn't your soul in more need of healing than your skin?"

—*The Mark of the King,* Jocelyn Green

When I call out, the Lord hears me. My prayer to the Lord is a healing balm for my soul.

MEDITATE ON PSALM 118:5

341 Time with My Creator

I wanted to be alone with the One. The One who scaled then careened from the heights of the mount. The One who raised up the man from the mud. The One who fashioned me from a part of the man and knew me more intimately than even the adam.

—Havah, Tosca Lee

I was made by the Master Creator, designed to be in communion with the Lord. I will spend time with my Creator each day.

MEDITATE ON GENESIS 2:21–23

---

342 Bold and Gentle Faith

She stood still. But she couldn't be at ease, not with that talk. "I'm not . . . " She had no reason to confess, did she? Except she had to. "I'm not what one would term religious. I realize you and Daisy are, but . . . "

. . . But Gwen smiled. "Our faith is the rock we stand on, Willa—but we don't demand anyone else stand here with us. Though if ever you wanted to, there is plenty of room."

—A Song Unheard, Roseanna M. White

Lord, give me boldness to share Your truth and hope with others, but to do so with gentleness and love.

MEDITATE ON ROMANS 1:16

---

343 God Is Still Here

"Margot." He lifted her hand and chafed her fingers between his equally cold ones. "God understands how you're feeling—that you're mourning, that you're angry, that you can't accept the way this has happened. But He's still there. His hand is still sheltering you. He'll wait for you."

—*The Number of Love,* Roseanna M. White

God understands all I feel, and still, the Lord never leaves me. I trust in the solid Rock that shelters me.

MEDITATE ON 2 SAMUEL 22:3

344 Pieces of My Heart

"You can't let yourself love because you think your heart can't handle it . . . that something bad will happen. But you're wrong. It's true . . . grief is the price for love. But hearts are made to mend. Christ can do wonders with a broken heart, if given all the pieces."

—*The Keeper,* Suzanne Woods Fisher

I have nothing to fear with God. I surrender the pieces of my heart to the Lord, full of faith that Christ will make something beautiful.

MEDITATE ON 1 CHRONICLES 28:20

345 For God's Glory

There were never any guarantees. Even being sure God wanted him to do this didn't mean he'd come home safely . . .

Sometimes God let people die. Let His children break. And then pieced them back together into something new. Something that He could use for His glory instead of theirs.

—The Number of Love, Roseanna M. White

God is glorified in my life! The ways of God are bigger than mine. I am shown grace through the wisdom of the Lord.

MEDITATE ON ROMANS 11:33–36

---

346 This Is the Prelude

I don't pretend to understand all of what happened. But I do know this—this right here is just prelude. Dress rehearsal. The intro. One of these days each one of us is going to get called up and given the chance to join our voices in a song we've never heard, yet one we've known our whole lives.

—Long Way Gone, Charles Martin

Our citizenship is clear in the Bible. I am a citizen of heaven for all time!

MEDITATE ON PHILIPPIANS 3:20

---

347 Pray First

"I'm uncomfortable with the resentment I see building between brothers and sisters in the Lord," he said softly. "How can Christ be honored through it?" I could see the pain in his dark brown eyes. "I appreciate the mediators who are trying to establish a dialog and work this out, but I'm convinced my place is one of prayer. God can do what man cannot."

—*Inescapable*, Nancy Mehl

Jesus is the true mediator. When I face a problem, I will go to the Lord, praying for wisdom to resolve all conflicts.

MEDITATE ON 1 TIMOTHY 2:5

348 Extend Grace

"So that guy over there, he's your bodyguard?"

"Yes."

"Looks like he has a rap sheet."

"He does." Mark spit. "I think all people have things in their past they need forgiveness for. In their present as well. And they need to be extended grace for what they regret."

—*The Chair*, James L. Rubart

I confess my sins to the Lord, grateful for the mercy given to me in forgiveness. I will show others the mercy of forgiveness.

MEDITATE ON 1 JOHN 1:7

349 Always with Me

I spent the next day packing and explaining to Charity why we had to move . . . I didn't want to worry her, but no matter how hard I fought to calm my fears, tears kept filling my eyes.

My grandmother's voice whispered inside me. **"There isn't anything too big for God, Lizzie girl. You gotta cast your cares on Him. He loves you so much."**

—*Inescapable*, Nancy Mehl

Nothing I face is too big or too small for God. The Lord cares about everything that affects me so I bring all my cares to the Father.

MEDITATE ON DEUTERONOMY 31:6

350 I Follow the Lord

"Well, sir, it just so happens that I have a warning for you as well." She got to her feet and stood her ground. "If I ever see you on this land again, I will not hesitate to report your trespassing and your threats of violence to the constable. This is my house and my farm, and I will house whomever I wish. I answer to God, and you would do good to remember that you will someday be called upon to answer to him as well."

—*We Hope for Better Things*, Erin Bartels

I follow the path God lays out for me. My eyes are steadfast on the Lord, and I stand firm with bold confidence in the ways of God in my life.

MEDITATE ON DEUTERONOMY 5:32–33

351 In the Image of God

"They are different in that they come from a god who says we are to show honor of him by honoring others. And so as we feed our hungry neighbor and do not steal from him we honor not our neighbor, but the image of the One who fashioned him. You say our god has no face. This is not true. Yaweh's face is before us in every person we see, as we are made in his image."

—*The Legend of Sheba*, Tosca Lee

We are all created in the image of the Living God, and we should love and honor one another as the Lord's beautiful creations.

MEDITATE ON GENESIS 5:1–2

352 Taking Up My Cross

"The point is to live—faithful each day." Curate Bauer looked as if he were speaking to a child. "And we must prepare and be prepared to go on living. Most of life is not high drama or danger. It is our responsibility to help those around us to live."

"Be our brother's keeper—that's what Friederich says."

"Or our sister's." He smiled. "Sometimes taking up our cross is doing the thing in front of us, not the glamorous, high-risk thing afar off."

—*Saving Amelie*, Cathy Gohlke

Lord, make my heart willing to do the next thing You put before me, whether it be big or small. I will do whatever You call me to do.

MEDITATE ON MATTHEW 16:24–25

353 To God Alone

Frank slipped a wooden toothpick out of his pocket and started to chew. "That's the problem when a man makes a stupid mistake. God forgives and we heal, but the consequences don't disappear."

"I think she put you on a pedestal because of how you cope with Mom and the Alzheimer's. You just got knocked off it."

"Well, good. I don't belong up there, and neither do you. No man does."

—*The Two of Us*, Victoria Bylin

I keep my eyes on God alone. No person is made to be worshipped. God alone is worthy of my devotion.

MEDITATE ON HEBREWS 12:2

---

354 For My Salvation

She nodded at last. "That's what they say Jesus did, isn't it?"

Curate Bauer's brows rose. "You understand, then."

"He probably didn't think that giving Himself up to be beaten and spit upon and crucified was very glamorous."

"For our sins. He did it for us because it was what we needed."

—*Saving Amelie*, Cathy Gohlke

Thank You, Jesus. Thank You for all You endured for my salvation. I am so grateful.

MEDITATE ON ROMANS 6:23

---

355 Carry the Load

"Each morning, when we wake—if we wake—we pick up whatever it is we've been given to carry for that day, with the sweet Lord Jesus in the yoke beside us to tote the load. Each night we lay it down, giving it into God's hands. If it's still there in the morning, we pick it up and begin again. If the burden is gone or if there is something different we know where to start."
—*Promise Me This,* Cathy Gohlke

I will walk side by side with the Lord, learning from the Father how to carry the load given to me each day.

MEDITATE ON MATTHEW 11:28–30

---

356 Mercy Over All

"Maybe your sin is much simpler. Maybe it's the ungodly attitude you show to others. Maybe it's unforgiveness you're holding in your heart. Maybe it's the way you're treating your spouse. Whatever it is, you know the Lord knows. We're going to deal with it this morning so we can put it away."

—*The Amen Sisters,* Angela Benson

Lord, I give You all my sins. You know my heart, the good and the bad, and Your mercy covers it all.

MEDITATE ON PROVERBS 28:13

---

357 God's Love Never Fails

*"We're imperfect human beings," Grand continued. "We're destined to fail. The only love that never fails is God's love. His love for his children—**us**—is boundless, battle-tested, and bold. It's trustworthy, tried and true. That kind of love requires action."*

—*The Two of Us,* Victoria Bylin

Father, help me understand the fullness of Your love toward me. Show me how endless Your love is in my life.

MEDITATE ON EPHESIANS 3:17–19

---

358 The Time Given Us

"I wish it need not have happened in my time," said Frodo.

"So do I," said Gandalf, "and so do all who live to see such times. But that is not for them to decide. All we have to decide is what to do with the time that is given us."

—*The Lord of the Rings,* J.R.R. Tolkien

The King of the World has given me this path to travel, and I can choose what to do with it. I choose to follow and live for the Lord with the time given to me!

MEDITATE ON ROMANS 14:8

---

359 We Have Directions

"I'm stuck here, I'm afraid."

"Well, that just ain't true dear, girl. No one's stuck anywhere unless they choose to be. The Lord God guides those who are moving forward." Such startling words . . . words that resonated in the depths of Joanna's heart.

—*The Bridesmaid,* Beverly Lewis

We are directed by the Voice of God telling us how to move forward. Try being quiet today and asking God to show you how to move forward.

MEDITATE ON ISAIAH 30:21

---

360 My Real Healing

*"I'm not . . . whole yet, Tony. But I cried out to God. Admitted
I needed help. Admitted that I hadn't dealt with the past. I was
honest with Him, just like you told me to be. And it was funny,
but just being real . . . started something. I guess when we're
genuine with God, then He can be genuine with us. Give us*
real *healing."*

—*Dark Deception*, Nancy Mehl

Lord, You are my healer. I bring my broken, wounded places to
You and cry out for Your help. I have complete faith in You.

MEDITATE ON LUKE 8:43–48

---

361 Building My Character

*"I'm sorry, Rosemarie." The duke crossed to me. "He didn't want
to speak with you, since the sheriff's confession was insulting.
But I encouraged him to see the task through to completion.
For it is often the hardest tasks that build the most character."*

—*An Uncertain Choice*, Jody Hedlund

Walking through hard things builds my character. I trust God
to give me the strength I need to be a person of integrity.

MEDITATE ON PROVERBS 27:19

---

362 It All Matters

Sarayu interrupted him. "Mack, if anything matters then everything matters. Because you are important, everything you do is important. Every time you forgive, the universe changes; every time you reach out and touch a heart or a life, the world changes; with every kindness and service, seen or unseen, my purposes are accomplished and nothing will ever be the same again."

—The Shack, William Paul Young

We are called to shine our light in the world. Today, I will do one thing to change the world for the better.

MEDITATE ON MATTHEW 5:14–16

---

363 My Eternal Story

"I understand now," he said. "Put it away! I am sorry: sorry you have come in for this burden; sorry about everything. Don't adventures ever have an end? I suppose not. Someone else always has to carry on the story."

—The Lord of the Rings, J.R.R. Tolkien

What I see here is not the end of my story. God has prepared a way for me to carry my story on into Eternity!

MEDITATE ON JOHN 14:1–3

---

364 The Presence of God

After that they didn't hurry so much and they allowed them-
selves more rests and longer ones. They were pretty tired by
now of course; but not what I'd call bitterly tired—only slow
and feeling very dreamy and tired as one does when one is
coming to the end of a long day in the open.
　　　　　　—The Lion, the Witch and the Wardrobe, C. S. Lewis

Rest is not wasted time in my life. God desires me to have rest
so I have time to experience the presence of the Lord.

MEDITATE ON EXODUS 33:14

---

365 Let God Carry It All

Instead of the usual cloud of depression that settled on her
when such thoughts came back, Alissa tried a new approach.
She had read in a devotional book that week, "When the devil
comes knocking on your door simply say, 'Jesus? It's for you.'"
Alissa mouthed the words, "Lord, I turn this over to you." It was
as if the black cloud stopped in midair and then evaporated.
　　　　　　　　　　　　　　—Sunsets, Robin Jones Gunn

The Lord will intervene and handle the things I cannot. I
entrust God with all the things that weigh me down with full
faith the Lord will carry them for me.

MEDITATE ON EXODUS 14:13–14

READING LIST

Afshar, Tessa. *Harvest of Gold.* Chicago: River North Fiction, 2013.

Afshar, Tessa. *Harvest of Rubies.* Chicago: River North Fiction, 2012.

Afshar, Tessa. *In the Field of Grace.* Chicago: River North Fiction, 2014.

Afshar, Tessa. *Land of Silence.* Carol Stream: Tyndale, 2016.

Afshar, Tessa. *Pearl in the Sand.* Chicago: Moody Publishers, 2010.

Alexander, Tamera. *A Lasting Impression.* Bloomington: Bethany House Publishers, 2011.

Alexander, Tamera. *Rekindled.* Bloomington: Bethany House Publishers, 2006.

Alexander, Tamera. *Within My Heart.* Bloomington: Bethany House Publishers, 2010.

Andrews, Mesu. *Love Amid the Ashes.* Grand Rapids: Revell, 2011.

Andrews, Mesu. *Love's Sacred Song.* Grand Rapids: Revell, 2012.

Andrews, Mesu. *Miriam.* Colorado Springs, WaterBrook Press, 2016.

Andrews, Mesu. *The Pharaoh's Daughter.* Colorado Springs, WaterBrook Press, 2015.

Austin, Lynn. *A Light to My Path.* Bloomington: Bethany House Publishers, 2004.

Austin, Lynn. *All Things New.* Bloomington: Bethany House Publishers, 2012.

Austin, Lynn. *Candle in the Darkness.* Bloomington: Bethany House Publishers, 2002.

Austin, Lynn. *Song of Redemption.* Bloomington: Bethany House Publishers, 2005.

Austin, Lynn. *While We're Far Apart.* Bloomington: Bethany House Publishers, 2010.

Austin, Lynn. *Wonderland Creek.* Bloomington: Bethany House Publishers, 2011.

Bartels, Erin. *We Hope for Better Things.* Grand Rapids: Revell, 2019.

Benson, Angela. *The Amen Sisters.* New York: Warner Books, 2005.

Benton, Lori. *A Flight of Arrows.* Colorado Springs: WaterBrook Press, 2016.

Benton, Lori. *Many Sparrows.* Colorado Springs: WaterBrook Press, 2017.

Benton, Lori. *The Pursuit of Tamsen Littlejohn.* Colorado Springs: WaterBrook Press, 2014.

Blackstock, Terri. *Last Light.* Grand Rapids: Zondervan, 2005.

Blackstock, Terri. *Seaside.* Grand Rapids: Zondervan, 2001.

Blackstock, Terri. *Truth Stained Lies.* Grand Rapids: Zondervan, 2012.

Blackstock, Terri. *Twisted Innocence.* Grand Rapids: Zondervan, 2015.

Bright, Bill, and Jack Cavanaugh. *Fire.* West Monroe: Howard Publishing Co., Inc. 2005.

Bunn, T. Davis, and Isabella Bunn. *The Innocent Libertine.* Bloomington: Bethany House Publishers, 2004.

Busse, Morgan L. *Daughter of Light*. Phoenix: Enclave Publishing, 2012.

Bylin, Victoria. *The Two of Us*. Bloomington: Bethany House Publishers, 2017.

Camden, Elizabeth. *The Lady of Bolton Hill*. Bloomington: Bethany House Publishers, 2011.

Camden, Elizabeth. *The Rose of Winslow Street*. Bloomington: Bethany House Publishers, 2012.

Camden, Elizabeth. *Until the Dawn*. Bloomington: Bethany House Publishers, 2015.

Chiavaroli, Heidi. *Freedom's Ring*. Carol Stream: Tyndale, 2017.

Chiavaroli, Heidi. *The Edge of Mercy*. Hope Creek Publishers, 2019.

Coble, Colleen. *Fire Dancer*. Nashville: WestBow Press, 2006.

Coble, Colleen. *Lonestar Secrets*. Nashville: Thomas Nelson, 2008.

Coble, Colleen, Kristin Billerbeck, Diann Hunt, and Denise Hunter. *Secretly Smitten*. Nashville: Thomas Nelson, 2012.

Coble, Colleen. *Silent Night: A Rock Harbor Christmas Novella*. Nashville: Thomas Nelson, 2012.

Connealy, Mary. *Deep Trouble*. Uhrichsville: Barbour Publishing, Inc., 2011.

Connealy, Mary. *Doctor in Petticoats*. Uhrichsville: Barbour Publishing, Inc., 2010.

Connealy, Mary. *Now and Forever*. Bloomington: Bethany House Publishers, 2015.

Connealy, Mary. *Petticoat Ranch*. Uhrichsville: Barbour Publishing, Inc., 2006.

Cossette, Connilyn. *A Light on the Hill*. Bloomington: Bethany House Publishers, 2018.

Cossette, Connilyn. *Counted with the Stars*. Bloomington: Bethany House Publishers, 2016.

Cossette, Connilyn. *Shadow of the Storm*. Bloomington: Bethany House Publishers, 2016.

Cossette, Connilyn. *Wings of the Wind*. Bloomington: Bethany House Publishers, 2017.

Dekker, Ted. *Blink of an Eye*. Nashville: Thomas Nelson, 2002.

Dekker, Ted and Erin Healy. *Kiss*. Nashville: Thomas Nelson, 2008.

Dekker, Ted. *Water Walker*. Brentwood: Worthy Publishing, 2014.

Dekker, Ted. *When Heaven Weeps*. Nashville: Thomas Nelson, 2005.

Dekker, Ted. *White: The Great Pursuit*. Nashville: Thomas Nelson, 2004.

Dickerson, Melanie. *The Fairest Beauty*. Grand Rapids: Zondervan, 2012.

Dickerson, Melanie. *The Merchant's Daughter*. Grand Rapids: Zondervan, 2011.

Dobson, Melanie. *Catching the Wind*. Carol Stream: Tyndale, 2017.

Dobson, Melanie. *Memories of Glass*. Carol Stream: Tyndale, 2019.

Dobson, Melanie. *Refuge on Crescent Hill*. Grand Rapids: Kregel Publications, 2010.

Dobson, Melanie. *Shadows of Ladenbrooke Manor*. New York: Howard Books, 2015.

Eason, Lynette. *Always Watching*. Grand Rapids: Revell, 2016.

Eason, Lynette. *Don't Look Back*. Grand Rapids: Revell, 2010.

Eason, Lynette. *When a Heart Stops*. Grand Rapids: Revell, 2012.

Eason, Lynette. *When a Secret Kills*. Grand Rapids: Revell, 2013.

Eason, Lynette. *Without Warning*. Grand Rapids: Revell, 2016.

Ella, Sara. *Unblemished*. Nashville: Thomas Nelson, 2016.

Endō, Shūsaku. *Silence*. New York: Picador, 1969.

Fabry, Chris. *Almost Heaven*. Grand Rapids: Tyndale, 2010.

Fabry, Chris. *Dogwood*. Grand Rapids: Tyndale, 2008.

Fabry, Chris. *War Room*. Grand Rapids: Tyndale, 2015.

Fisher, Suzanne Woods. *The Keeper*. Grand Rapids: Revell, 2012.

Fisher, Suzanne Woods. *The Search*. Grand Rapids: Revell, 2011.

Frantz, Laura. *Love's Reckoning*. Grand Rapids: Revell, 2012.

Frantz, Laura. *The Mistress of Tall Acre*. Grand Rapids: Revell, 2015.

Ganshert, Katie. *A Broken Kind of Beautiful*. New York: WaterBrook Press, 2014.

Ganshert, Katie. *Life After*. New York: WaterBrook Press, 2017.

Ganshert, Katie. *The Art of Losing Yourself*. New York: WaterBrook Press, 2015.

Ganshert, Katie. *Wildflowers from Winter*. New York: WaterBrook Press, 2012.

Garlough Brown, Sharon. *Sensible Shoes: A Story About the Spiritual Journey*. Downers Grove: InterVarsity Press, 2013.

Gohlke, Cathy. *Band of Sisters*. Carol Stream: Tyndale, 2012.

Gohlke, Cathy. *Promise Me This*. Carol Stream: Tyndale, 2012.

Gohlke, Cathy. *Saving Amelie*. Carol Stream: Tyndale, 2014.

Green, Jocelyn. *A Refuge Assured*. Bloomington: Bethany House Publishers, 2018.

Green, Jocelyn. *The Mark of the King*. Bloomington: Bethany House Publishers, 2017.

Green, Jocelyn. *Wedded to War*. Chicago: Moody Publishers, 2012.

Gunn, Robin Jones. *Sunsets*. Colorado Springs: Multnomah, 1997.

Hancock, Karen. *The Shadow Within*. Bloomington: Bethany House Publishers, 2004.

Hatcher, Robin Lee. *A Matter of Character*. Grand Rapids: Zondervan, 2010.

Hatcher, Robin Lee. *Belonging*. Grand Rapids: Zondervan, 2011.

Hatcher, Robin Lee. *Fit to Be Tied*. Grand Rapids: Zondervan, 2009.

Hatcher, Robin Lee. *Heart of Gold*. Nashville: Thomas Nelson, 2012.

Hatcher, Robin Lee. *Love Without End*. Nashville: Thomas Nelson, 2014.

Hatcher, Robin Lee. *The Perfect Life*. Nashville: Thomas Nelson, 2008.

Hatcher, Robin Lee. *Wagered Heart*. Grand Rapids: Zondervan, 2008.

Hauck, Rachel. *A March Bride*. Grand Rapids: Zondervan, 2014.

Hauck, Rachel. *Love Starts with Elle*. Nashville: Thomas Nelson, 2008.

Hauck, Rachel. *Once Upon a Prince*. Grand Rapids: Zondervan, 2013.

Hauck, Rachel. *The Love Letter*. Nashville: Thomas Nelson, 2018.

Hauck, Rachel. *The Memory House*. Nashville: Thomas Nelson, 2019.

Hauck, Rachel. *The Wedding Dress*. Nashville: Thomas Nelson, 2012.

Hedlund, Jody. *An Uncertain Choice*. Grand Rapids: Zondervan, 2015.

Hedlund, Jody. *Hearts Made Whole*. Bloomington: Bethany House Publishers, 2015.

Hedlund, Jody. *The Preacher's Bride*. Bloomington: Bethany House Publishers, 2010.

Hedlund, Jody. *Undaunted Hope*. Bloomington: Bethany House Publishers, 2016.

Hedlund, Jody. *Unending Devotion*. Bloomington: Bethany House Publishers, 2012.

Heitzmann, Kristen. *Secrets*. Bloomington: Bethany House Publishers, 2004.

Heitzmann, Kristen. *The Rose Legacy*. Bloomington: Bethany House Publishers, 2000.

Henderson, Dee. *Danger in the Shadows*. Carol Stream: Tyndale, 1999.

Henderson, Dee. *Taken*. Bloomington: Bethany House, 2015.

Henderson, Dee. *The Guardian*. Carol Stream: Tyndale, 2001.

Henderson, Dee. *The Healer*. Carol Stream: Tyndale, 2002.

Henderson, Dee. *The Protector*. Carol Stream: Tyndale, 2001.

Henderson, Dee. *The Rescuer*. Carol Stream: Tyndale, 2003.

Henderson, Dee. *Unspoken*. Bloomington: Bethany House Publishers, 2013.

Hunt, Angela Elwell. *A Time to Mend*. Steeple Hill Books, 2006.

Hunt, Angela Elwell. *Bathsheba*. Bloomington: Bethany House Publishers, 2015.

Hunt, Angela Elwell. *Egypt's Sister*. Bloomington: Bethany House Publishers, 2017.

Hunt, Angela Elwell. *The Note*. W Publishing Group: Nashville, 2001.

Hunt, Angela Elwell. *The Velvet Shadow*. Colorado Springs: WaterBrook Press, 1999.

Hunter, Denise. *A December Bride*. Grand Rapids: Zondervan, 2013.

Hunter, Denise. *Barefoot Summer*. Nashville: Thomas Nelson, 2013.

Hunter, Denise. *Driftwood Lane*. Nashville: Thomas Nelson, 2010.

Hunter, Denise. *Falling Like Snowflakes*. Nashville: Thomas Nelson, 2015.

Hunter, Denise. *On Magnolia Lane*. Nashville: Thomas Nelson, 2018.

Hunter, Denise. *The Goodbye Bride*. Nashville: Thomas Nelson, 2016.

Hurnard, Hannah. *Hinds' Feet on High Places*. Blacksburg: Wilder Publications, 2010.

Isaac, Kara. *Then There Was You*. Bellbird Press, 2017.

Jackson, Neta. *The Yada Yada Prayer Group*. Nashville: Thomas Nelson, 2003.

Jenkins, Jerry B. and Chris Fabry. *Grave Shadows*. Carol Stream: Tyndale, 2005.

Jenkins, Jerry B. *Though None Go with Me*. Grand Rapids: Zondervan, 2000.

Karon, Jan. *A Light in the Window*. New York: Penguin Group, 1995.

Karon, Jan. *A New Song*. New York: Penguin Group, 1999.

Karon, Jan. *At Home in Mitford*. New York: G.P. Putnam's Sons, 1995.

Karon, Jan. *Come Rain or Come Shine*. New York: G.P. Putnam's Sons, 2015.

Karon, Jan. *Home to Holly Springs*. New York: Penguin Group, 2007.

Karon, Jan. *In This Mountain*. New York: Penguin Group, 2002.

Karon, Jan. *Somewhere Safe with Somebody Good*. New York: Berkley, 2014.

Kingsbury, Karen and Gary Smalley. *Redemption*. Carol Stream: Tyndale, 2007.

Kingsbury, Karen. *Angels Walking*. New York: Howard Books, 2014.

Kingsbury, Karen. *A Time to Embrace*. Nashville: Thomas Nelson, 2002.

Kingsbury, Karen. *Between Sundays*. Grand Rapids: Zondervan, 2007.

Kingsbury, Karen. *Ever After*. Grand Rapids: Zondervan, 2006.

Kingsbury, Karen. *Fifteen Minutes*. New York: Howard Books, 2013.

Kingsbury, Karen. *Gideon's Gift*. Warner Books, 2002.

Kingsbury, Karen. *Like Dandelion Dust*. New York: Hachette Book Group, 2006.

Kingsbury, Karen. *Loving*. Grand Rapids: Zondervan, 2012.

Kingsbury, Karen. *Oceans Apart*. Grand Rapids: Zondervan, 2004.

Kingsbury, Karen. *The Chance*. New York: Howard Books, 2013.

Klassen, Julie. *The Ladies of Ivy Cottage*. Bloomington: Bethany House Publishers, 2017.

Klassen, Julie. *The Secret of Pembrooke Park*. Bloomington: Bethany House Publishers, 2014.

Klassen, Julie. *The Silent Governess*. Bloomington: Bethany House Publishers, 2009.

LaHaye, Tim, and Jerry B. Jenkins. *Nicolae*. Carol Stream: Tyndale, 1997.

LaHaye, Tim, and Jerry B. Jenkins. *Rapture's Witness*. Carol Stream: Tyndale, 2009.

LaHaye, Tim, and Jerry B. Jenkins. *The Indwelling: The Beast Takes Possession*. Carol Stream: Tyndale, 2000.

Laureano, Carla. *The Saturday Night Supper Club*. New York: Tyndale, 2018.

Lee, Tosca. *Havah*. Nashville: B & H Publishing Group, 2010.

Lee, Tosca. *The Legend of Sheba*. New York: Howard Books, 2014.

L'Engle, Madeleine. *A Wind in the Door*. New York: Square Fish, 1973.

L'Engle, Madeleine. *A Wrinkle in Time*. New York: Square Fish, 1962.

Lewis, Beverly. *The Bridesmaid*. Bloomington: Bethany House Publishers, 2012.

Lewis, Beverly. *The Ebb Tide*. Bloomington: Bethany House Publishers, 2017.

Lewis, Beverly. *The Fiddler*. Bloomington: Bethany House Publishers, 2012.

Lewis, Beverly. *The Judgement*. Bloomington: Bethany House Publishers, 2011.

Lewis, Beverly. *The Prodigal*. Bloomington: Bethany House Publishers, 2004.

Lewis, C. S. *The Lion, the Witch and the Wardrobe*. New York: Harper Collins, 1950.

Linden, Rachel. *The Enlightenment of Bees*. Nashville: Thomas Nelson, 2019.

Lucado, Max. *Miracle at the Higher Grounds Café*. Nashville: Thomas Nelson, 2015.

Marshall, Catherine. *Christy*. Grand Rapids: Evergreen Farm, 1967.

Marshall, Catherine. *Julie*. Wheaton: Evergreen Farm, 1983.

Martin, Charles. *Chasing Fireflies*. Nashville: Thomas Nelson, 2007.

Martin, Charles. *Long Way Gone*. Nashville: Thomas Nelson, 2016.

Martin, Charles. *The Mountain Between Us*. New York: Broadway Books, 2010.

Martin, Charles. *Thunder and Rain*. New York: Hachette Book Group, 2012.

Martin, Charles. *Water from My Heart*. New York: Center Street, 2015.

Martin, Charles. *When Crickets Cry*. Nashville: WestBow Press, 2006.

McGee, Stephania H. *Missing Mercy*. Brandon: By the Vine Press, 2019.

Mehl, Nancy. *Dark Deception*. Bloomington: Bethany House Publishers, 2017.

Mehl, Nancy. *Fatal Frost*. Bloomington: Bethany House Publishers, 2016.

Mehl, Nancy. *Inescapable*. Bloomington: Bethany House Publishers, 2012.

Miller, Calvin. *The Singer*. Downers Grove: Intervarsity Press, 1975.

Moore, Beth. *The Undoing of Saint Silvanus*. Carol Stream: Tyndale, 2016.

Oke, Janette. *A Searching Heart*. Bloomington: Bethany House Publishers, 1998.

Oke, Janette. *Love's Long Journey*. Bloomington: Bethany House Publishers, 1982.

Oke, Janette. *Once Upon a Summer*. Bloomington: Bethany House Publishers, 1981.

Parrish, Christa. *Still Life*. Nashville: Thomas Nelson, 2015.

Parrish, Christa. *Stones for Bread*. Nashville: Thomas Nelson, 2013.

Peretti, Frank E. *Monster*. Nashville: West Bow Press, 2005.

Peretti, Frank E. *This Present Darkness*. Wheaton: Crossway Books, 1986.

Petersheim, Jolina. *The Alliance*. Carol Stream: Tyndale, 2016.

Peterson, Tracie. *A Lady of Secret Devotion*. Bloomington: Bethany House Publishers, 2008.

Peterson, Tracie. *A Matter of Heart*. Bloomington: Bethany House Publishers, 2014.

Peterson, Tracie. *An Unexpected Love*. Bloomington: Bethany House Publishers, 2008.

Peterson, Tracie. *Dawn's Prelude*. Bloomington: Bethany House Publishers, 2009.

Peterson, Tracie. *Hearts Aglow*. Bloomington: Bethany House Publishers, 2011.

Peterson, Tracie. *Morning's Refrain*. Bloomington: Bethany House Publishers, 2010.

Peterson, Tracie. *The Icecutter's Daughter*. Bloomington: Bethany House Publishers, 2013.

Peterson, Tracie. *Twilight's Serenade*. Bloomington: Bethany House Publishers, 2010.

Peterson, Tracie. *Where My Heart Belongs*. Bloomington: Bethany House Publishers, 2007.

Pettrey, Dani. *Dead Drift*. Bloomington: Bethany House Publishers, 2018.

Pettrey, Dani. *Sabotaged*. Bloomington: Bethany House Publishers, 2015.

Pettrey, Dani. *Silenced*. Bloomington: Bethany House Publishers, 2014.

Pettrey, Dani. *Submerged*. Bloomington: Bethany House Publishers, 2012.

Pettrey, Dani. *The Killing Tide*. Bloomington: Bethany House Publishers, 2019.

Phoenix, Michèle. *The Space Between Words*. Nashville: Thomas Nelson, 2017.

Reay, Katherine. *A Portrait of Emily Price*. Nashville: Thomas Nelson, 2017.

Rivers, Francine. *As Sure as the Dawn*. Carol Stream: Tyndale, 1995.

Rivers, Francine. *Redeeming Love*. Colorado Springs: Multnomah Books, 1997.

Rivers, Francine. *The Masterpiece*. Carol Stream: Tyndale, 2018.

Rubart, James L. *The Chair*. Nashville: B & H Publishing Group, 2011.

Rubart, James L. *The Five Times I Met Myself*. Nashville: Thomas Nelson, 2015.

Ruchti, Cynthia. *As Waters Gone By*. Nashville: Abingdon Press, 2015.

Ruchti, Cynthia. *They Almost Always Come Home*. Nashville: Abingdon Press, 2010.

Ruchti, Cynthia. *When the Morning Glory Blooms*. Nashville: Abingdon Press, 2013.

Rue, Nancy N. and Stephen Arterburn. *Healing Sands*. Nashville: Thomas Nelson, 2009.

Rue, Nancy N. and Stephen Arterburn. *Healing Stones*. Nashville: Thomas Nelson, 2007.

Rue, Nancy and Stephen Arterburn. *Healing Waters*. Nashville: Thomas Nelson, 2008.

Rue, Nancy. *False Friends and True Strangers*. Grand Rapids: Zondervan, 2003.

Rue, Nancy. *Tristan's Gap*. Colorado Springs: WaterBrook Press, 2006.

Singer, Randy. *Fatal Conviction*. Carol Stream: Tyndale, 2010.

Smucker, Shawn. *The Day the Angels Fell*. Grand Rapids: Revell, 2017.

Smucker, Shawn. *The Edge of Over There*. Grand Rapids: Revell, 2018.

Snelling, Lauraine. *A Land to Call Home*. Bloomington: Bethany House Publishers, 1997.

Snelling, Lauraine. *Valley of Dreams*. Bloomington: Bethany House Publishers, 2011.

Stuart, Kelli. *Like a River from Its Course*. Grand Rapids: Kregel Publications, 2016.

Tolkien, J.R.R. *The Lord of the Rings*. New York: Del Rey, 1954.

Wade, Becky. *A Love Like Ours*. Bloomington: Bethany House Publishers, 2015.

Wade, Becky. *My Stubborn Heart*. Bloomington: Bethany House Publishers, 2012.

Wade, Becky. *True to You*. Bloomington: Bethany House Publishers, 2017.

Wade, Becky. *Undeniably Yours*. Bloomington: Bethany House Publishers, 2013.

Warren, Susan May. *Duchess*. SDG Publishing, 2017.

Warren, Susan May. *Happily Ever After*. Carol Stream: Tyndale, 2003.

Warren, Susan May. *It Had to Be You*. Carol Stream: Tyndale, 2014.

Warren, Susan May. *Licensed for Trouble*. Carol Stream: Tyndale, 2010.

White, Roseanna M. *A Song Unheard*. Bloomington: Bethany House Publishers, 2018.

White, Roseanna M. *The Number of Love*. Bloomington: Bethany House Publishers, 2019.

Whitlow, Robert. *Deeper Water*. Nashville: Thomas Nelson, 2008.

Whitlow, Robert. *Higher Hope*. Nashville: Thomas Nelson, 2009.

Whitlow, Robert. *Mountain Top*. Nashville: Thomas Nelson, 2006.

Whitlow, Robert. *The List*. Nashville: Thomas Nelson, 2000.

Wick, Lori. *A Gathering of Memories*. Eugene: Harvest House Publishers, 1991.

Williamson, Jill. *Captives*. Grand Rapids: Zondervan, 2013.

Williamson, Jill. *From Darkness Won*. Phoenix: Enclave Publishing, 2011.

Wingate, Lisa. *The Prayer Box*. New York: Tyndale, 2013.

Wingate, Lisa. *The Story Keeper*. New York: Tyndale, 2014.

Wright, Jaime Jo. *The Reckoning at Gossamer Pond*. Bloomington: Bethany House Publishers, 2018.

Young, William Paul. *The Shack*. Newbury Park: Windblown Media, 2007.

TOPICS

SCRIPTURE INDEX

ACKNOWLEDGMENTS

Every day, I started this project with a simple prayer:

Lord, help me focus well and do this project for Your glory. Show me what to include and help me put it on the page boldly. May You be honored and glorified in the writing, editing, and publishing of these words. Thank You for giving me all I need to do Your work. Amen.

I am so grateful that God heard and honored my prayer every step of the way. From the grace given by my family to the wisdom and encouragement from the team of people behind this book, I have been blessed.

There are many people that made it possible for you to read these meditations:

The team at Callisto Media who gave opportunity, vision, and wisdom along the way, making this entire project possible, thank you. Especially Adrienne Ingrum, Virginia Bhashkar, and Daniel Grogan, who made these words shine.

My friends who cheered me on to keep putting words on the page for the glory of God. Jenny, Christine, Jennifer, and Sondra helped me believe in myself and, better yet, in my God.

My parents who taught me what faith and love look like, and my siblings who make me laugh and drive me crazy. I'm so glad they're mine.

Eliza, Timothy, and Annalise, who teach me what the love of a parent is and inspire me to chase my dreams, giving all their love along the way. They are my heart.

Andrew, the love of my life, who believes in me, supports me, and picked up the slack so I could put these words on the page for the glory of God. All my love, forever.

And to the Father, who answered my simple prayer and offers me grace upon grace all of my days.

ABOUT THE AUTHOR

REBECCA HASTINGS believes in finding extraordinary grace in ordinary life. As a writer and speaker, she encourages people to look beyond Sunday morning to discover faith every day. She is the author of *Worthy: Believe Who God Says You Are* and has been featured in the *Washington Post* and *RELEVANT* magazine. She lives with her husband, three kids, and two dogs in Connecticut. Rebecca can often be found typing words, driving her kids places, or wherever there is chocolate. Connect with her at www.rebeccahastings.net.

CPSIA information can be obtained
at www.ICGtesting.com
Printed in the USA
BVHW020759230220
573064BV00017B/372

9 781641 528740